RAY COMFORT

OUT *of the* COMFORT ZONE

The Authorized Autobiography

Bridge-Logos
Alachua, Florida 32615 USA

Bridge-Logos Publishers
Alachua, FL 32615, USA

Out of the Comfort Zone
by Ray Comfort

Edited by Lynn Copeland

Copyright © 2003 by Ray Comfort

Cover, page design, and production by Genesis Group
(design@genesisbebsite.com)

Printed in the United States of America

ISBN 978-0-88270-943-7

Library of Congress Card Catalog Number: 2007927623

Unless otherwise indicated, Scripture quotations are from the *New King James* version, ©1979, 1980, 1982 by Thomas Nelson Inc., Publishers, Nashville, Tennessee.

Scripture references marked KJV are from the *King James Version.*

Originally published under the titles *My Friends Are Dying!* and *The Power of Darkness.* Includes the previously published *Miracle in the Making.*

G163.319.B.m904.35230

CONTENTS

To my brother, Phillip,
and Mark and Laura Spence

FOREWORD

Ray Comfort is a little man on a big mission. I don't know whether to call him a lunatic, a man on fire for the Lord, or just a normal, biblical Christian. Traveling with Ray is like trying to keep up with a five-year-old boy in a toy store—every time I turn around, he's gone! Just when I'm sure he's exhausted every possible opportunity to speak with people about eternal life, he's found another one. A police officer, a desk clerk, a passenger, a waiter. In airports, hotels, and restaurants; on airplanes and elevators; even in public restrooms—anywhere! We've come close to missing flights, being arrested, and getting punched out, all because Ray won't quit.

The wonderful thing about watching him in action is seeing the wake of smiles he leaves behind. What a thrill to see long lines of people waiting to board their planes reading "$1 million bill" tracts, laughing at the "World's Funniest One-Liners," and even going out of their way to ask him for more for their friends. In all my years of learning about God and His wonderful ways, I have never met anyone from whom I've learned as much, or with whom I've been so grateful to spend time, as this little lunatic from New Zealand named Ray Comfort.

Kirk Cameron

CHAPTER 1

A PLACE of DEATH

H e's got a knife!" I couldn't believe my eyes. This wasn't television—it was *real life.* Chuck hadn't been able to come to the park at the last minute, leaving me with Beth, a gentle nurse, and my teenage daughter, Rachel, as helpers. As we were giving out food to a long line of park residents, I was distracted by the shouting. I lifted up my eyes to see a slim man in his early twenties being chased by a much bigger man, who was holding a seven-inch blade at arm's length as he ran. The potential stabbee was literally running for his life. The scene reminded me of those animal programs showing a sleek antelope being chased for dear life by a powerful leopard. The terrified animal darts back and forth, while the intent pursuer follows with purpose in his graceful, speeding step. His one objective: the jugular vein of his prey.

7

The pursuer I was watching had that same look in his eye as his victim fell into the dust beneath his feet. He lifted the shining blade for the kill. Rachel turned her head away at the thought of someone being stabbed to death before her eyes. Time froze. During those seconds, as the man stood over his helpless victim, his friends were able to grab both of his arms until the blinding spirit of murder lifted from his mind.

As suddenly as it had begun, it was all over. The dust settled; the terrified antelope quickly picked himself up out of the dirt and ran. The leopard wrestled free from those who held him, then walked back to the group he came from, no doubt to do more "business." I carefully eyed him. He was tall, clean, and reasonably well-dressed. When he emerged from the group with food in his hand, he began eating as though nothing had happened.

This "place of death" was the famed MacArthur Park, commonly known as the "Armpit of L.A."

I felt a mixture of shock and anger at witnessing such drama. While I was grappling with my emotions, a man who was waiting patiently for his food—which was still in my hand— breathed out, "This is a place of death."

This "place of death" was the famed MacArthur Park, commonly known as the "Armpit of L.A."—and quite rightly so. It had the grisly reputation of having the highest crime rate in the entire Los Angeles area. It was the hideout of prostitutes, pimps, thieves, drug dealers, addicts, alcoholics, murderers, the destitute, and the homeless. After half an hour in the park, I saw more drugs than I'd seen in my whole life.

I was, however, very familiar with the drug scene. Back

in June 1975, in Christchurch, New Zealand, a friend named Ron visited our home while I was out, and left a message with my wife, Sue. When I returned, Sue told me, "Ron's a nice sort of fellow. He needs $70 for a radio he bought off some guy; can we spare it?" Ron had made a Christian commitment a few weeks earlier. He'd been on the hard stuff for over six years and had come clean.

"Sure," I replied. "Where's the checkbook?" Ron stopped by for the money later that afternoon and we arranged to go to a surf movie that night. I would pick him up at 7 p.m. at "Hood Street."

The Hood Street apartment, about half a mile from our house, was the hangout for the local surfers when there was no surf. I'd never been there. I owned the area's only surf shop and normally didn't mingle with the guys after hours. Now was my opportunity to see how they lived. I knew a number of them were playing around with dope, and some were into the acid scene. This worried me because I had seen a radical character change in a couple of friends. It was as though life was slowly draining out of them. They lost interest in surfing and became withdrawn.

Hood Street

I entered the apartment and sat down on an unmade bed in a small room. As I waited for Ron, I looked around and noticed a couple of syringes, spoons, and some matches on a small, brown table in the middle of the room.

Suddenly, my thoughts were interrupted by a knock at the door, which was quickly opened by Russell, the guy who had let me in. In came four familiar faces. The newcomers cautiously greeted me then looked back at Russell. "He's okay," Russell grinned. A few more locals came through the door and within seconds the place was a hive of activity. Plastic syringes were recovered from various hiding places—under beds, in suitcases, in between books, and even from the front of underwear.

With another knock at the door, the activity stopped and the hive became deadly silent. *"Who is it?"*

"It's me, Greg!"

The door opened and in staggered Greg, looking pale and holding onto his stomach. "Did you score? *My gut is killing me!"*

Russell pointed to the table where there were two small, white Palfium tablets. A smile of relief came across Greg's face as he asked how the day had gone.

"Great!" said Russell. "We scored from three doctors." He then turned to me and explained that Palfium is a synthetic heroin. If an addict wanted to get off heroin, all he had to do in those days was convince a doctor that he meant business, and he would get a prescription for fifty or so tablets, which were to be taken orally. If these were instead crushed and injected, they gave a great "flash"—as good as the real thing. These guys spent the whole day going through the phone book, noting which doctors were easy to score from. Russell said he would never go to old Dr. Cook again. "He got me on my knees and prayed for me with tears in his eyes—*man, that was too much!"*

Meanwhile, another four youths entered the room. Pills were being crushed, mixed with water, and heated on a spoon over a lit match. Then the mixture was carefully poured into a hypodermic needle. I was both fascinated and horrified. Someone took off his leather belt. Jeff, who was about twenty-five with a solid build, was the first to use it. He stood up, wrapped the belt loosely around his forearm, and began to swing his arm round and round like some sort of human helicopter. Then, when the blood rushed to his forearm, he pulled the belt tight to hold the blood in place. He started on the inside slowly moving up his wrist, searching for a good vein. I watched in revulsion as he pushed the needle into a faint blue line, but even with the belt wrapped tightly around the arm, the vein wouldn't rise. After a string of profanity, he muttered, "It's no good—these have had it!"

Out came the needle, held in a now shaking hand, and in it would go again about an eighth of an inch to the left. Blood would spring up and be quickly wiped away with a communal handkerchief. In again, a quarter of an inch to the right. More cursing. Off came the shoe and sock. There it was—a superb blue vein, just below the ankle. In went the needle . . . and out went the liquid.

A sigh of relief came as Jeff dropped the needle onto the table and lay back on the bed, hands on his forehead as he waited for the "rush."

"Let's hold Ray down and give him a shot," joked Russell. I managed to return a smile and told them not to waste it on me.

Lifetime Marriage

Meanwhile, Ron had been out back of the apartment. He came in and greeted me, then we went outside and hopped into my car. After about two miles, he asked if we could stop. When he got out and threw up on the curb, I thought it had something to do with the diabetes he had because of his drug addiction.

However, as we sat in the surf movie that night, I could feel the bench we were sitting on shaking. Ron was trembling from head to foot. *He was back into drugs,* I thought, bitterly disappointed. I learned later that one of his drug friends was watching his progress to see if there was any hope for his own terrible drug problem. When hearing of Ron's nosedive, he wept. If Ron could make it, so could he...but his only hope had crumbled before his eyes. For many, once the needle goes in, it's a lifetime marriage—'til death do us part.

Around the time I found out that Ron was back into the drug scene, Dr. Cook dropped into my surf shop and congratulated me on the work I had been doing with the local drug addicts. He opened his diary and showed me about a dozen names of guys I had never heard of, with whom I was supposedly working. They had been using my name to hoodwink Dr. Cook into believing they were trying to get off drugs!

Within a few years, the Hood Street crowd dissipated.

For many, once the needle goes in, it's a lifetime marriage—'til death do us part.

Mark went to South Africa and got into some bad opium. One smoke put him in a mental institution for two and a half years. Doctors recorded that he managed only seven words in twelve months. Mike spent three years in mental institutions. He advanced from Palfium to ransacking medical cabinets and chewing whatever he could lay his hands on.

I went to John's funeral. His sister was lying across his coffin screaming his name. He was killed in a fight over drugs. Some guy smashed a beer bottle in half and thrust it into his groin, severing an artery. His friends couldn't stop the bleeding. As his life's blood drained from his body, he was able to ask that farewells be given to his family.

Greg rode his motorbike while he was high and was killed in a crash. He was nineteen. Rodney and Tom went to prison for selling LSD. Tim used heroin and alcohol together, and died of heart failure; he was twenty. Jim's girlfriend found him dead on the bathroom floor. He died after twenty-nine days of constipation caused by the Palfium. Jan committed suicide while on LSD by jumping off a two-hundred-foot cliff.

My smiling friend Russell moved on to barbiturates, then into the occult. He ended up getting twelve years in prison for murdering a man in his late twenties by cutting off both of his hands with a machete.

After getting out of prison, he was killed in a motorcycle accident.

CHAPTER 2

SPEAKER'S CORNER

I've often been told that I've lived a charmed life. I guess that means things seemed to work out for me in life. Compared to most other people, I did have a very happy childhood. Other than being bullied in school, visiting the dentist when they had the "slow drill," seeing my dog killed on the road, and breaking my arm while playing football, there wasn't much to scar my memory. Up until I was twelve years old, life was nothing more than building huts, raiding orchards, and playing wars.

At the age of thirteen I obtained a Saturday morning job as a bricklayer's helper. It was cold, hard work but I stayed with the job for six months, until I had enough money to buy my own surfboard. From then on I spent every available minute on my board.

At the age of sixteen, a rich aunt paid for my brother,

Phillip, and me to take a cruise from New Zealand to Tahiti and Fiji. The trip was a double blessing because it also got me out of school for two whole weeks. I wasn't too happy about sitting in a classroom when the surf was up. All I wanted to do was ride waves, and all the school wanted to do was fill my head with knowledge that I thought I would never use. When I graduated, I was so delighted to leave, I threw my bag of school books about twenty feet into the air and let them crash to the ground.

> *Despite my intelligence, my striking good looks, and my humility, Sue wasn't interested in me.*

I then began working in a bank. It was there that I saw my future wife for the first time. Unfortunately, the attraction was one-way. Despite my intelligence, my striking good looks, and my humility, Sue wasn't interested in me. However, one day she was asked by her boss to take some papers across town. I quickly offered to transport her on my motorbike and, to my surprise, she accepted.

I will never forget the thrill of having her wrap her arms around me and hold on tight (something I suggested for safety's sake). From then on she began greeting me as I returned from spending my daily lunch hour surfing.

One day I saw one of my surfing heroes wearing a fringed "cowboy" jacket. It looked so cool that I decided to make one for myself. I spent thirty hours hand-sewing a rough suede jacket, and so enjoyed making it that I made another five and hung them in my bedroom. One day a carload of surfers showed up and bought three. I then made more, found an empty store, and rented it for a day. The jackets sold quickly, so I decided to quit my bank job and open a combination surf shop and Leathergear store, in which I made over 1,500 jackets and coats to order during a ten-year period. I advertised that you could have a jacket or coat made to order "while you wait." You had to wait about three months.

A New Sound

It was during this time that Sue and I were married. We saw a house for sale not far from our business (and half a mile from the beach), so we purchased it for the grand sum of $5,300. It wasn't exactly a mansion, but it was clean and cute, and we loved it. We loved it so much that we were on our honeymoon only one day before we sneaked back to be in our little Comfort Inn.

About a year after we were married, Jacob was born. I was with Sue the entire time she was in labor and was so overwhelmed by the miracle of childbirth, I wept.

A year or so later, another baby arrived—our daughter, Rachel. At that time we had a friend who was deeply involved in a breast-feeding organization, who believed that if your teenager didn't rush home from school and jump onto his mother's breast, she was sinning against God and not being the woman she should be. These sincere (though well-meaning) folks encouraged us to "demand feed" our newborn. That meant that when the baby cried, we should feed her. So we did. Every time. If the mouth opened, we happily filled it.

This gave us a baby who was as wide as she was high. Her cheeks looked like she had two whole oranges in her mouth. Our darling daughter turned into a monstrous, screaming, demanding, milk-drinking machine, and the "demand" was on Sue. She became drained, not only of milk, but also of her health (I would lie awake at night frustrated that male nipples were merely ornamental). We decided to secretly transfer our baby to the bottle so that I would be able to help Sue.

Even though the bottle helped, we were still being woken from sleep eight to ten times each night by the screams of a demanding baby. So we secretly invested in a pacifier, and slipped it into the slot. That seemed to be the missing link in the evolution of our child. For two whole nights we slept peacefully... until a new sound entered our lives. It went something like this: *Yawyawyawyawyawyawyaw...ping!* It was the depressing sound of a pacifier becoming boring.

Then some helpful soul suggested, "Put honey on the pacifier," so we did. That worked for two nights, until we were woken by the dreaded and now familiar *yawyaw...ping.* It was the sound of *honey* becoming boring. We fell back into the routine of eight to ten nightly pilgrimages into the baby's room.

I will never forget my joyful deep sleep being suddenly broken by a sinking feeling upon hearing the dreaded *ping!* I would mechanically rise and sleepwalk toward the noise, leaving the light off so as not to awaken myself too much. I knew the direction in which the missile had been fired, so I would feel on the floor for the pacifier. I would then pull the carpet-fur from the teat and search in the dark with my hand for the saucer of honey. Often my fingers found their way into the middle of the saucer. One dip of the pacifier, and into the baby's mouth. Sort of. It often took a few trial-and-error attempts. In the morning her cheeks looked like a piece of worn-out carpet.

This went on for weeks, until we finally took her to a specialist. To our dismay, he told us that we had a perfectly healthy, well-fed baby. (We had hoped there was something wrong that could easily be righted.) She was parent-made.

Some months later we took her to a dentist. She needed a filling in her front baby-tooth, because the constant sucking of the honey had created a grand canyon.

Rachel grew up to be a slim, sweet (and tolerant) daughter, who learned a lot about when to feed a baby from her parents' mistakes.

A few years after Rachel, Daniel was born. The first night we had him home he screamed around midnight. When Sue started to get out of bed to feed him, I simply said, "Remember Rachel!" She immediately lay back down, and we listened to him cry for about thirty minutes and then went back to sleep. He's been fine since.

The Chinese Shuffle

During the first year of our marriage, for some reason I picked up a huge rock on a beach and ended up with a hernia. My doctor felt the small egg-shaped lump, and then advised me to have an operation.

When I arrived at the hospital, I noticed a number of elderly men doing what I called "the Chinese shuffle." When I asked why the men were walking as though they were wearing loose slippers, I was told that they had had hernia operations. I remember thinking, *I am twenty-one years old, at the prime of my life, and there is no way I am going to walk like that!*

A few hours later I awoke after the operation, amazed that no time seemed to have passed from the moment I lost consciousness on the operating table until I awoke in the bed. I was conscious of one thing, though. I needed to go to the bathroom, so I carefully slid off the bed and placed my feet firmly on the floor. However, the moment I tried to take a step, an atomic bomb went off in my lower abdomen. I had never felt such intense pain. I had to wait ten minutes to humble myself and ask for a nurse to help me back into bed. *I couldn't even manage the Chinese shuffle!* Neither could I cough, laugh, or sneeze.

As soon as I realized that I shouldn't laugh, almost anything set me off into painful hysterics. I had to keep a screen around my bed because the mere glance of other patients set me off. Visitors were warned not to make me laugh, so they would enter my area with a strained look on their face that sent me into such agonizing hysterics, I ended up in tears.

It became such a problem that the doctor decided to send me home three days early.

Even at home, Sue would find herself walking into our bedroom with a tray of food for me, setting off the laughter for no reason, and having to do a U-turn. I ended up taking more than ninety painkillers that week.

The change in my life was radical. It was a shock to my friends— and to me.

The experience was a powerful lesson. It humbled me, and brought me to the realization that it doesn't take much to bring any of us to a place of utter weakness and dependence on others. In retrospect, I suspect that God's hand was in that circumstance, preparing me for the message that only the humble will hear.

Doormat Ministry

About two years after we were married, I was converted to Christianity (which I will mention in more detail in a later chapter). The change in my life was radical. It was a shock to my friends—and to me. Five of us went on a surfing trip talking of the usual things guys talk about, and three days later, back we came...*singing hymns.*

Two weeks after my conversion, a 91-year-old Presbyterian minister named George Densem came into my leather/surf shop, shook my hand, and congratulated me on my conversion. From that moment on we became the best of friends.

One day George insisted that he buy me a $90 "Gestetner"—a hand-cranking machine used for copying (before the photocopier became popular). I suppose the Lord was leading him, because I had no idea why he did that. I typed out a tract about the root cause of racial problems—that it was sin, not skin—and cranked out a hundred or so on the primitive Gestetner. Someone saw the tract and ordered 5,000 copies. That was the humble beginning of our tract ministry, which now sells millions of tracts each year.

After visiting Hood Street and seeing the condition of some of the people I'd met, I decided to open a rehabilitation center. I rented an old house and put a large sign on the roof: The One and Only Way.

The house was ideal as it had a good-sized room for Bible studies among other things. Two nights after my conversion, we had started a home Bible study group that became too big for our living room. The new premises became a place where those who had been in the drug world could stay to make a clean break from their drug-using friends. It was also somewhere I could work. Soon after my conversion, I had dedicated the surf shop/leather store to God and found myself evicted a month later. I continued to make custom leather jackets in our home for several months until the local authorities found out. Much to my dismay, they wouldn't allow me to use a commercial sewing machine in a residential area, so The One and Only Way had a threefold purpose: business, Bible study, and boardinghouse.

It wasn't long before I became very disillusioned with drug rehabilitation. Anyone who tries to help those in the drug scene is going to be lied to and stomped on. Ron's $70 was just the beginning; drugs and deceit go hand-in-hand.

The climax came when I found a coffee cup filled with blood in the kitchen. Our new "drug-free Christians" had been cleaning their paraphernalia in the drinking mugs.

That incident, among other things, was the end of the rehabilitation center. I closed the house and moved my leather business into the heart of our city, six miles away.

If Only

One day I remember giving Sue the car and taking a bus to work. As I looked closely at all the faces of my fellow travelers, I thought, *Every one of them is going to die. How I wish I had the courage to stand up and tell them I have found the answer to death!* At the same time, I could envision the vehicle screeching to a halt, and all the passengers in unison throwing me off the bus. *If only there was somewhere I could speak to people…if only.* That was a radical request. For years I suffered from what is commonly called an inferiority complex. In elementary school I was nicknamed "Red Indian" because I blushed at the drop of a hat. In fact, even if the hat didn't drop, I blushed. One question from the teacher directed at me caused Red Indian to rear his ugly head. I would then (without fail) hear someone say, "Why are you turning red?" The same question plagued my mind—why *was* I turning red?

Red Indian chased me like an enemy through high school and fatally wounded me one Tuesday morning. Each Tuesday four or five students had to make a class speech. The thought of humiliating myself in front of my peers terrified me. So when it came to my turn alphabetically, I stayed away from school. The trouble was, the teacher diligently crossed off every name on the list except mine. One black Tuesday, *my number was up.*

I stood up and spoke on the subject of surfing, something I could talk about for hours on a one-to-one basis.

There was nothing like it. I so loved it, I objected if it was referred to as a sport. It was a way of life, a freedom that those who didn't surf had no idea about. I would just share my heart... the joy of surfing.

After about thirty seconds, I became very conscious of the sound of my own voice, as though I had never heard it before. Then began the dreaded sound of my heart, beating in my chest like an Indian war drum... then that dreaded hot flush to my face... and the blank mind. I was humiliated beyond words. I stopped halfway through my speech and sat down. Custer had nothing on me. That was my last stand. Never, *never* would I stand up and speak in public again! Never.

So it was radical for me to think, *If only there was somewhere I could speak to these people.*

Shortly after the bus incident, a colorful character dressed as a wizard (and calling himself "the Wizard") arrived in our city of 350,000 and embarrassed the town council. The law stated that no one was allowed to speak to crowds in the open air, so he set up a chalkboard and, rather than speaking, he gave people the written word.

The news media loved it and followed the story with great interest. After two weeks of pressure, the authorities designated an area in the heart of the city for public speaking and called it "Speaker's Corner."

When that happened, I thought to myself, *What an answer to prayer... horrors!* I avoided the place like the plague, until I saw a picture in the newspaper that seemed to jump out and slap my face. Under the picture, it explained that an elderly, violin-playing woman was speaking about her faith to groups of people in the local square. I felt ashamed, and determined to go into the Square and speak to the crowd.

Ironically, it was a Tuesday on which I found myself facing

a group of people in Speaker's Corner. There was no pounding heart, no hot flush, no humiliation...just plain old terror. But, with the help of God, I broke out of my comfort zone and spoke that day. Little did I know that it would be the first of three thousand times.

Some might ask why anyone would want to open-air preach. This may be because they have an image of a fiery-eyed fanatic, standing on a street corner holding a sign that reads "You're going to hell!", and yelling at passersby who (understandably) are passing by as quickly as possible. If that's the typical picture of an open-air preacher, I wouldn't blame anyone for being reticent about the subject. However, while there were times of heated debate at Speaker's Corner, it was a wonderful opportunity to spread the claims of the gospel in a uniquely inoffensive fashion. After all, Jesus, Paul, Peter, Stephen, Spurgeon, Wesley, Whitefield, D. L. Moody, Billy Graham, and many others were open-air preachers. If it is done in the right spirit, a good open-air preacher can reach more people in half an hour than the average church does in half a year.

As much as we would like it to happen, fish don't jump into the frying pan. You have to actually *go* fishing. And sinners don't readily come to buildings we call "churches." They avoid them.

My Friends Are Dying!

It was during those early days of open-air speaking that I attended the funeral of the fifth Hood Street friend who died from drug abuse. The sight of John's sister lying across his coffin, screaming out his name, left an indelible impression on my mind. I felt frustrated that so many were being cut off in their youth, so I produced an eight-page pamphlet on the dangers of drug abuse and called it "My Friends Are Dying!"

A charitable trust heard of my endeavor and gave me $1,000 to have more printed to get them into schools. Soon after that came the printing of a book with the same name. I stayed up almost all night for three nights to finish the publication and took it to my printer. I had been using D. N. Adam's Printing Company to publish a paper called "Living Waters" for a few years. We didn't advertise, the papers were free, and we didn't ask for money. Sometimes we would find money stuffed in our mailbox, placed on our doorstep, or tossed through our bedroom window. Every time the printing bill was due, the funds were there to pay it.

I asked the manager of the company how much it would cost to print a book. He said it would be around $3,000, so I told him that I would raise the money and come back. He replied, "There's no need. I know where you get your money from. Pay us when it sells."

I was in a quandary about how to get publicity for it, as I couldn't afford to advertise. One day the subject came up when I was speaking to my friendly rival, the Wizard (whose photo appeared in the book). He spoke once a week on a popular radio program, "cursing" different things around the country. I quietly suggested, "Why don't you curse my book?" He smiled, said with his raspy voice, "Now that's a good idea," and took a copy with him.

The following Tuesday I turned on the radio at 8 a.m. and heard, "Ray Comfort's book is crudely written. It has photos of me in it, without my long hair and beard. The publication is pathetic. It's called *My Friends Are Dying!*, and you will find it for sale at..." and he named the bookstore. They completely sold out that morning!

From then on the book received national media attention and opened up an itinerant ministry for me. I began getting hundreds of invitations to speak at schools, churches, and service groups. After speaking on drug prevention, I gave a basic gospel message.

Shortly after its publication I opened the Drug Prevention Center, which was located on High Street—an unfortunate choice of street names for a drug center. This was different from the rehabilitation center. Our aim this time was to *prevent* drug abuse through education, rather than trying to clean up the mess at the other end.

One day I looked up and saw a couple in their mid-twenties looking at books on the shelves. They turned out to

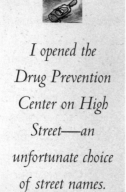

I opened the Drug Prevention Center on High Street—an unfortunate choice of street names.

be addicts who were curious about what I was doing. Jeff was quiet and reserved, but Mary was very outgoing. In fact, she reminded me of an "everybody's girl" in an old western saloon. While I was speaking to them, a call came from a television station wanting to interview me about how drugs were smuggled into prison. That morning, an addict had been found dead on his cell floor from a drug overdose. I agreed, but when I put the phone down I thought, *How on earth do they get drugs into prison? What have I gotten myself into!*

It was then that Jeff and Mary filled me in on how to get drugs past the prison authorities, subtle ways such as putting LSD under the stamps on mail or injecting oranges with narcotics.

I shared my faith with them and gave each a New Testament. Mary took it gratefully and even asked me to write my name in it. As she left that day, I saw her spin around in a dance of elation as she left. She was so warm and full of life.

It seemed I'd made another friend.

Two weeks later I received a call. "This is the police department. We have found a couple of bodies in an apartment. One, a female, has a New Testament on her with your name in it. Would you come down and identify the bodies?" I almost injured my fist as I punched the wall in frustration.

Gang Odor

As I spoke in Speaker's Corner, I could see familiar faces of the gangs that hung around the Square. The leader, "Baldie," sure looked the part, with his strong, prairie-bare head of an Indian chief. As I looked at him, I thought, *How can I befriend these guys?* Just then someone came up to me, shook my hand, and left $20 in it.

I walked up to Baldie and asked, "How would you guys like some lunch?" He looked shocked and muttered, "All of us?" I told him I would buy lunch for the whole gang, and instructed him to follow me. I ran ahead to ask the manager of a local eatery if he minded me bringing the whole gang for a feed, but before I could get to him, in they came, carrying with them their own familiar aroma.

From that time on, Baldie and friends came to visit me regularly at the Drug Prevention Center. I loved to see them. In fact, I felt proud of the friendship I had with these rejects of society. Unfortunately, the surrounding tenants didn't feel the same way. They pressured the landlord, who then gently but firmly pressured me to vacate the premises. Rather than break my friendship with the gang, I decided to seek another building.

After looking at a number of prospects, I noticed a large dome-shaped structure five stories high in what was known as the Regent Theater Buildings. It seemed ideal as it overlooked the area where I preached in Speaker's Corner. Three of us made some inquiries, found who had the key, unlocked the door and went inside.

It was perfect! I knelt down and prayed, "God, if you are in this, please let me know." Then I jumped to my feet and ran back with the key. As I entered the man's office, I said, "I will take that Dome if that's okay with you," to which he replied, "Fine, but you will have to contact the owner. His name is Mr. Godbehere." *Godbehere!* Two minutes earlier I had prayed, "God, if you are in this, please let me know"!

A few days later I received a telegram, "Renting of the Dome approved . . . *Godbehere.*"

God certainly was there. Because of my speaking engagements and counseling, instead of making five jackets a week, I was turning out only one. But every month, without us making our needs known, money came in for the rent. In fact, it was the exact amount we needed every month for twelve months (except for one, when it was ten times the amount), at just the right time each month.

Then something happened that did more than rock my boat. It tipped me out completely.

CHAPTER 3

LOOK NORTH

I t was 6:30 a.m. on November 5, 1979. I never like being wakened by the telephone, because it takes me some time to think straight. This morning was different. I was thinking as clear as a bell after hearing the words, *"Ray, the whole Regent Theater Building is on fire!"*

This was no hoax. In no time at all I was looking at smoke pouring from the building. Fire trucks and police surrounded the area. As I gazed at the Dome, a Christian friend came up to me and said he had been watching earlier when the fire started and immediately began praying for the Dome to be protected.

It truly was. Not one thing was even singed, while all the surrounding buildings were nothing but a blackened mess.

That night I got out of bed to read my Bible. I needed to know what was going on. I had been reading through the

Book of Ezekiel and opened my Bible to chapter 8. My eyes widened as a number of words seemed to leap from the page: "On the fifth day of the month...I looked, and there was...the appearance of *fire...fire...*lift up your eyes now *toward the north...toward the north...*" It seemed that God not only knew about my situation, but that a door would someday open toward the north. That was encouraging because there was nothing much *south* of New Zealand except penguins.

Three days later a friend approached me as I was about to speak in the Square and said: "Good verse, that one in Revelation—'I know your works. See, I have set before you an open door, and no one can shut it; for you have a little strength, have kept My word, and have not denied My name.'" It seemed to confirm that someday a door would open "toward the north."

Over the next few weeks, I continued going into the Drug Prevention Center as usual. As I clambered over the still wet and smoky stench of the charred remains of the Regent Theater Buildings to get to my place of work, I wondered if God wanted me to move on. The fire seemed to have taken the heat out of the ministry.

When my pastor asked if I would pray about going into full-time ministry with our church, I hardly needed to. The offer was an answer to prayer. However, I had the good sense to pray about the situation, and it seemed that God even gave me a verse to direct me. It was one Bible verse that came alive as I was reading Scripture: "Study to show thyself approved unto God" (2 Timothy 2:15, KJV).

I was asked to be an assistant pastor in our church, which had grown from a handful of people to around 250. The peace I felt in my heart, coupled with 2 Timothy 2:15, was all I needed to make the transition from Drug Prevention Director to Pastor Ray Comfort. I was excited at the thought.

There was one small setback. When I closed my ministry to become an assistant pastor, I found that "Pastor's Assistant" had been placed on the door of my office. Some perceptive church member had crossed out the "istant" so that the sign read "Pastor's Ass."

For the next three and a half years, that's what I was: the pastor's gofer. Although disappointed that I was never referred to as a pastor, I was careful to watch my attitude.

The pastor's lack of faith in me was a sign of a deeper problem he had. From the moment he was hired, he hardly trusted a soul. In fact, all the elders of the church left because of his insecurity, leaving us with a church full of young people who didn't have the maturity to realize that something was radically wrong. Someone once complained that there were no elders in the church. I relayed the complaint to him, and he said, "Of course there are—there's you and me."

We did clash in one area. I felt that church members should spend more time with their wives and fam-

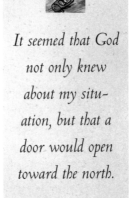

It seemed that God not only knew about my situation, but that a door would open toward the north.

ilies. He didn't think so. In fact, he arranged a campaign of meetings over a Christmas period. We had twenty-six meetings in ten days, and I was expected to be at every meeting.

One night shortly after that, his wife ended up on our doorstep in tears. It seemed that the pastor didn't spend much time with her and their four daughters.

The next day, I tried to encourage him to take some flowers home to his wife, to which he replied, "There are plenty in the garden."

The pastor also had a close relationship with his secretary. I didn't give much thought to the friendship until I looked back on it months later.

The Pain of the Pastorate

After my three and a half years of hard labor, churches began to invite me to speak on how Christians could share their faith. I was thrilled to set aside pastoral work—which was something I didn't enjoy at all. I found counseling professing Christians to be a waste of time. They would come in for marriage counseling, then after I poured my heart out for twenty minutes, I would find that they were actually living in adultery.

So many speaking invitations began to come in that I decided to leave the church. Sue and I opened a Christian bookstore to supplement our income. The change was actually a relief. With the lack of mature leadership in the church, and the clash between what the pastor and I viewed as important, our relationship had become a little strained. Soon after, Sue and I decided to attend another church, one closer to the heart of our city. They took me on staff, without pay, as an itinerant minister.

Not long after our move to the new church, the pastor of our old church committed adultery with his secretary, and left his wife and four children. He then threatened to sue the church if they didn't give him a certain amount of pay when he left.

There was one big highlight during those difficult years. I embarked upon the making of a thirty-minute documentary film titled *My Friends Are Dying!* I had made an 8 mm production, and felt confident that I could handle the making of a 16 mm film. I knew someone who had been trained in filmmaking, and when I asked him to help me, he was excited about the idea. Although the book had received much publicity, I wondered who would bother to come to see a Christian anti-drug film. It needed something as a drawing card. With this thought in mind, I sent John, my camera-man, into the Square to get some candid shots of people in the crowd, while I went to a luncheon.

When I arrived at the Square, my friend the Wizard said to me, "You sure missed something today. While I was speak-ing, a gang fight, with axes and knives, broke out, *and a TV cameraman got the whole thing on film!*" I asked if the man was about 5'9" with black curly hair. He said he was, so I rushed to John's house, and sure enough, he had captured the whole sequence on film. That night the police came and seized the footage to use as evidence against the gangs.

Sadly, John had been so shaken by what he had captured on camera that he neglected to film the police arrival after the fight, so the next day I called the police and asked if they would consider arriving again. The officer in charge said, "You scratched our back by giving us the film, so we will scratch yours."

The following day we had the interesting experience of filming two squad cars weaving in and out of traffic as they sped down the main street. Then they screeched to a halt, and four police officers tore open their car doors...*and rushed into an empty square!*

The police had no trouble rounding up the guilty par-ties. They had all the evidence on film. The irony was that Baldie and his gang were put in prison for their part in the fight, all because of my movie.

After police returned the film containing the fight se-quence, I was able to complete the documentary. The pastor of a large church in the center of the city volunteered his building for its premiere as it could hold 1,200 people. The building was filled to capacity during the initial screening. In fact, over 1,000 people had to be turned away—including the pastor, who couldn't get in!

Stay Where You Are

A few months later, I was asked to screen the film at a local prison. I was a little apprehensive because I knew that Baldie and his gang would be there, and I wondered what their attitude would be toward the guy responsible for their imprisonment.

Authorities told me that there would be three screenings so the prisoners would be easier to manage. I was allowed ten minutes to speak to the prisoners after each screening.

After the first session the men became noisy and began getting up to leave. Suddenly, a large guard hollered, "Stay where you are! Mr. Comfort is gonna speak to you!" They immediately quieted down and listened to every word I said.

After the second screening, the same thing happened. This time Baldie stood up and butted in while I was speaking. He was angry. I found out later that he wasn't mad because the film had put him in prison, but because it didn't clearly show his gang as being victors in the fight.

As the third screening came to an end, I looked around for my big guard. He was nowhere to be found. When the movie finished and the men stood up to leave, I jumped to my feet, took a deep breath and hollered, "Stay where you are. I'm gonna speak to you!" Not a soul moved.

CHAPTER 4

IT TOOK SO LONG *to* BAKE IT

For many years, I had the privilege of speaking in hundreds of churches from almost every denomination. People would often ask if my itinerant ministry made it difficult for the family. They presumed that I was away from home most of the year. Not so. I limited my travel to two or three weekends each month. That meant that sometimes I would have two weeks uninterrupted with Sue. It also meant that I was able to spend a lot of time with the kids. We would often walk together through a local forest (there are no bears, snakes, lions, crocodiles, or deadly spiders in New Zealand) and catch tadpoles and frogs. I would wade neck deep into a pond and scoop frogs into a handheld net when they surfaced to see what was happening in the upper world. We had a small pond in our backyard, complete with a diving board for the captured frogs. We sold the frogs for a few dollars each, and raised $200 spending money for the kids. Sue would often stay at home while the kids and I went on these adventures, so I took great delight in buying a hot, roasted chicken, and halfway into the forest sitting beneath a tree with my offspring and eating chicken without feminine etiquette.

One memorable incident was when the four of us had been circling a pond for some time. If you have even seen a frog on the edge of a pond or in the water, you will know how difficult it is to catch one. If his head is above the water and he sees you make one movement, he is gone in an instant, diving to the bottom of the pond and burrowing in the mud. If he is on the edge and detects you coming, you will hear a tiny "plop" as he dives into the water with such precision and so little splash that he would take the gold and any Olympic event. Frogs are masterpieces of God's incredible genius.

To catch one frog a day was a success. Two was revival. However, this day was totally frog-less. After some time, Daniel (our youngest) said, "We will *never* catch a frog today. It's impossible." I turned to him and said, "Daniel, never use that word. With God, nothing shall be impossible." We caught five frogs in less than an hour that day!

The First Part

Weekend travel around our country had become a way of life. Sue and I no longer needed our bookstore to supplement our income. Life was sweet—no counseling, no clashes with the pastor. But things were about to radically change.

The pastor of our church called us into his office. We talked for two hours on different subjects. He was a kind, loving man who had a true pastor's heart. He had allowed me to speak from the pulpit a number of times, and he seemed to appreciate what I had to say. However, on one occasion, after I had finished speaking at the church, he took the microphone and much to my shock said, "I totally agree with everything Ray had to say...in the *first* part of his sermon."

In my many years of speaking, this was the only time something like this had happened. I had said that the Church as a whole had become lukewarm in its convictions toward the lost and had lost sight of its agenda. I pointed to the fact that when eight pastors in a small nation such as ours get cancer and die (despite widespread fasting and prayer for their healing), something is radically wrong.

Life was sweet—no counseling, no clashes with the pastor. But things were about to radically change.

When I had shared the same message at the largest church in the country a few weeks earlier, almost the entire congregation streamed to the altar to seek God and ask for His forgiveness. Not so in my home church. They didn't get a chance to respond.

However, it seemed that incident had been forgotten. The meeting Sue and I were having with him was very congenial.

Suddenly he said, "Of course, I can't continue to give my covering for your ministry..." Then he changed the subject and carried on in his friendly manner, closed in prayer, and we left.

I was devastated! His words echoed in my mind: "I can't continue to give my covering for your ministry." What on earth did the future hold for a preacher whose pastor had wiped his hands of him?

Within an hour of arriving home after the meeting, we received a call from Pastor Garry Ansdell of Hosanna Chapel in Bellflower, California. I had heard from him a number of times previously. He explained that he had been studying what I had to say through my books and tapes, then he said, "America *must* hear this message. We feel that God is directing us to offer our covering for your ministry. Would you come and bring this message to the Church of the U.S.?"

My pastor had taken his covering off my ministry, and now, less than two hours later, a pastor in the United States was offering his covering. Something was definitely going on.

A Strange Sight

I had met Garry Ansdell while ministering in Hawaii about a year prior to the call. When I was introduced to him, God seemed to say to my heart, "This man will be instrumental in opening doors to the United States."

The next day I gave him something I had written. As he read it, he initially disagreed with its content. Then he began to search the Scriptures on the subject and saw that what I was saying was biblical.

A few months after our meeting, he invited me to speak at his church in California. Sue went with me, and we both began to feel a real closeness to Garry and his family. This was partly because he was enthusiastic when I had suggested doing an outreach in the open air. He even volunteered to get into a gorilla suit that I had, to draw a crowd. When I began speaking at the base of the pier at Huntington Beach, Garry lay on the ground (in the gorilla suit) under a white sheet. As a crowd gathered, I talked about the fact that each of us has to die eventually. Then I pulled the chain that was around the gorilla's neck. Up jumped the pastor, and I spoke about the theory of evolution.

He was so excited that he even got up on my soapbox after I finished, and spoke to the crowd himself. That thrilled me because for the twelve years in which I had spoken almost daily in my hometown, it seemed that local pastors had avoided the Square.

When he asked if we would consider moving to the U.S., I said we would make it a matter of prayer. Leaving New Zealand would mean that we would have to leave our home and our families, and I would have to uproot from my open-air preaching ministry. Leaving the Square wouldn't be easy. Although we were aware that sometime in the future God would open a "door to the north," we didn't think it would come so soon.

Come Before Winter

The day following Garry's call, Sue was reading her Bible when a Scripture seemed to jump from the page. The next day, we received a letter from the United States, and that same very obscure, but applicable Bible verse was written across the letter. We decided that we had better sit on our patio and list the prophecies given to us over the years, specifically the many I had been given about a "door" opening to the north.

One that came to mind was when a visiting minister who had called me out of the congregation laid his hand on my head and began to quietly pray. Then he began to laugh. He kept laughing for a full sixty seconds, then said, "Oh, the joy of what I am seeing. *This is wonderful.* I see thousands of young people...and *you* are leading them. This is wonderful!"

Another incident came to mind. Three pastors fasted for three days and sought God's direction for our congregation. As one of the men prayed for me, he said, "God is going to use you in conducting funerals. He is going to open doors in Australia, England, Israel, and the United States." (Since that time, I have conducted scores of fake open-air funerals to draw a crowd and have spoken in each of these places.)

As Sue and I sat on the patio with pen in hand, we saw a strange sight. A balloon, unaided by human hand, suddenly appeared over our back fence. It rose to a height of about eight feet, then moved horizontally until it was almost directly in front of us. It was such a strange spectacle, I ran up to it and noticed that it had a picture of a rainbow on it. The balloon, still unaided by human hand, then slowly sank down into the neighbor's property. While we weren't exactly ready to pack our bags because of a balloon, we were aware that a rainbow is indicative of God's faithfulness.

As I left that day to preach in the Square, I told Sue that something would come in the mail to direct us. It did. In the mail we received a book from someone who had no idea of our situation. It was titled *Come Before Winter and Share My Joy*, written by a pastor who lived in Los Angeles.

Sue told me later that the balloon didn't remain on our neighbor's property. After I left, it began to slowly lift. She watched it get higher and higher in the sky, until it disappeared into the heavens.

Cake in the Rain

I prayed about where I would preach if we moved to a city like Los Angeles. Did they have an open square? Did they allow public speaking? How would I find out these things? These thoughts ran through my mind as I arrived in the New Zealand city of Rotorua to speak at a Christian camp. I stared out the window as the plane taxied toward the terminal, aware that it was probably the last time I would speak there.

I could never get used to being met at airports, mainly because most of the time I didn't know who was going to meet me. As I walked into the terminal, I tried to look as much like me as I could. After a short time, a lean man in his late thirties approached me and said my name questioningly in an American accent. I smiled and nodded in response. As we made our way to the baggage claim area, we made small talk about the flight.

As the talk got larger, I asked him what part of America he was from. It turned out that he was from Los Angeles. I was amazed, because of all the people to meet me at the airport, here was an American, way "Down Under" in New Zealand. But more than that, it was someone from the *Los Angeles* area. I asked him what specific part of L.A. he was from since the Los Angeles area includes about one hundred cities. His answer stunned me: "Bellflower." That was the very city we had been invited to! This man was a Godsend.

I told him of my concerns about where I would preach the gospel. It had to be outdoors, somewhere I could go daily —a place where plenty of people gathered. His answer was immediate: "The only place I know of is MacArthur Park. It was used in the sixties for public speaking during the Vietnam War protests." I was familiar with the name; the park was immortalized by the hit song of the late sixties, "MacArthur Park," sung by Richard Harris. Over the weekend at the camp, this Christian brother was able to give me valuable advice on the do's and don'ts of life in the United States.

After arriving back in Christchurch, I couldn't get the "MacArthur Park" melody out of my mind. I hadn't heard the song for at least ten years, and it was amazing that I could still remember the words. They were rather strange: "Someone left the cake out in the rain...and it took so long to bake it...and I'll never have the recipe again...oh no..."

With the song still echoing through the corridors of my mind, I turned on the radio to listen to the news. What I heard first were the last three bars of a song. I stood there in disbelief; *it couldn't be!* My train of thought was interrupted by the DJ saying, "Fantastic! Richard Harris, MacArthur Park..."

Shortly after that, I met another American at a New Zealand airport, so I grilled him about the park and found that it wasn't as exciting as the name sounded. In fact he told me not to go there at night because I could be murdered. When he said that it was the abode of the dregs of humanity, I immediately thought of taking sandwiches with me to give to the homeless.

Three months passed. Time had completely tucked the "MacArthur Park" incident into the back of my mind. I was wondering if there would be someplace closer to Bellflower where I could preach. MacArthur Park was in downtown L.A. and looked like it would be a thirty- or forty-minute drive each way. Once again, those strange words started coming to mind, "Someone left the cake out in the rain..." I turned on the TV and again, unbelievably, I heard that same song on television—*the second time I had heard it in ten years, both times just after I had been singing the tune.*

Late in 1988, I decided to lay down my ministry "Down Under." I wept the night I knew God was going to take us away from our home, our families, and everything we loved so dearly. Yet He had been preparing our hearts for some time.

We decided to tell our parents of our conviction that God seemed to be leading us to live in the U.S. I was very apprehensive about telling Sue's mom and dad about such a radical move. When we did tell them, her father smiled. Two days earlier he had remarked to his wife that he thought God would move us to America. Although my mom wasn't exactly excited about us leaving, she too said that God had prepared her two days earlier, by putting the thought in her mind that we would go to live in the United States.

These incidents confirmed that God was leading us, so we decided to sell our home. We didn't even get it onto the market. *It sold to the very first person I mentioned it to.* During that time, other odd events happened. A friend who had listened to me speak for years suddenly called out my name as I was leaving the Square. He ran up to me, shook my hand and said soberly, "Good-bye." He knew nothing of our situation, and had never done such a thing before. It was strange.

What's Shane's Number?

During the years of preaching open-air in the Square, I had been blessed and plagued by hecklers. Blessed because a good heckler drew a crowd of two hundred in a matter of minutes. Plagued because some of my hecklers drew the crowd, but would not let me speak to them. Many of these were what are commonly called "backsliders." They are people who make a "decision for Christ" but "fall away" from the faith. "Backslider" is actually an unscriptural word to describe them, because they didn't slide forward in the first place. They had a *false* conversion. Usually they come to Christ for the wrong reason—to have a drug or alcohol problem solved, to have a broken marriage fixed, to get rid of loneliness, or maybe to find happiness or peace. It's not long before they are disillusioned. Christianity promises four things: tribulation, temptation, persecution, and everlasting life. Those who return to their old lives count themselves unworthy of eternal life. What's more, they often become so bitter that they daily, week after week, month after month, year after year, hound a certain open-air preacher.

One of these hecklers was a man named Tom. He was about 6'2", and was apt to shake with anger when heckling me. He would curse, mock, and blaspheme the name of Jesus almost daily. He would even spit on me (or *at* me, depending on the wind direction), such was his contempt for the gospel. Yet there was something likable about Tom. He would say things like, "You've got authority over me. Why?

Why is it that I feel you have authority over me?" Over lunch I told him why. The demons in him were under the authority of the Holy Spirit in me.

Not only did I like Tom, but I felt sorry for him because he was a typical casualty of modern evangelism. The gospel he had heard was the false gospel of promised happiness. When things didn't fall into place as the evangelist had told him, he became disillusioned and *very* bitter. Much of his disillusionment was justified. He mocked the greed of many churches and the superficial emotionalism that characterizes many altar calls.

"Lord, I really don't want to go back to pastoring, but if that is Your will, I will gladly heed Your call."

Tom couldn't believe that I accepted him, and more than that, loved him. I had to show him that my concern was more than just words. After talking it over with Sue, we decided to give him our car when we moved.

For the next three months, I felt excitement well up within me at the thought of giving him our vehicle. Every time he spat, either verbally or literally, I couldn't help beaming at the thought of how he was going to feel when he realized that I still liked him.

Strange though it may sound, it's very hard for a proud person to accept a car as a gift. I thought that this might be the case with Tom, so the day we were due to leave New Zealand, I called him over, gave him the keys and quietly told him the car was his. After some deliberation, he shook his head and said that the thought was nice, but there was no way he could take it.

He handed back the keys and walked off. As he did so, I called out, "What's Shane's phone number?" Shane was another nasty heckler. Tom and Shane hated each other. He turned and said, "*You wouldn't give it to Shane!*" I handed him the keys and left, beaming.

It Would Drive Me Crazy

"Come here now, Daniel!" I made sure that my voice sounded gruff. Within seconds, my youngest son would be standing obediently in front of me, and I would say, "I'm pleased you came straight away. I have a candy bar for you." I enjoyed seeing if my ten-year-old would obey me even when he didn't understand why I was calling him.

It had been about five years since I had left pastoring. Since that time, I had been speaking throughout New Zealand and overseas and had an established itinerant ministry. One day I saw the Christian brother who had so accurately prophesied about how I would be used in the administration of funerals and about a number of other things that had come to pass. He looked at me and said, "God is going to call you back to being a pastor." I smiled and quietly shook off his words. The last thing I wanted to do was to go back to being a pastor and speaking to the same people week after week...after week. I would drive them and myself crazy. My heart was for evangelism, not for teaching and counseling Christians.

A month or so later I saw his car following mine. When I parked the vehicle, he parked across the street. He walked up to me and said resolutely, "God is going to call you back to being a pastor!" Again I dismissed his words from my mind.

That night I got up for prayer and yielded myself to God. I said, "Lord, I *really* don't want to go back to pastoring, but if that is Your will, I will gladly heed Your call."

Shortly after Sue and I accepted the invitation to move to the United States, the immigration department required the church to specify the capacity of my employment. As I held the fax they sent me, my eyes fell upon my new job title: "pastor of evangelism." God had called me with a "gruff" voice to see if I would obey Him. Now He had a candy bar for me.

As we left our home to head for the U.S., I gazed at a beautiful rainbow that spanned the sky. Our area of the country had been in a drought for months. It was the first rainbow I had seen for a long time, and it was very special. It was as though God was reminding us of His faithfulness— that our faithful Creator was directing this move, big though it was for us.

When we arrived in California in January 1989, one of the first things Garry Ansdell did, not knowing the details of my experiences, was give me a ring. Inscribed in it were the words "Pastor Ray Comfort." Also inscribed was "2 Tim. 2:15," the same verse God impressed upon me years earlier when I began full-time ministry with our church.

CHAPTER 5

MacArthur Park

In February, a friend and I headed out to try some open-air preaching in Los Angeles. As we rounded the corner, there it was—the famed MacArthur Park. With its green grass and tall palm trees surrounding a large lake, it was scenic postcard material...from a distance. As we got closer, I could see groups of people holding fistfuls of cash and throwing dice on the ground. I grabbed my soapbox from the car and walked around them, telling my friend that I preferred to explore the park and see if there was somewhere else I could speak. I was a little nervous. I suspected that the gamblers wouldn't be too congenial to the preaching of the gospel.

The other side of the park was none too friendly either. In fact it looked like a place where the dregs of humanity came. It reeked of urine and was filthy with piles of trash strewn around the ground. I made the mistake of glancing into the public restrooms. It was my first and last glance. I had never seen anything like it in all my life. If those restrooms had been situated down at the beach, the tide wouldn't have come in.

I placed the soapbox on the ground about twenty feet in front of a group of rough-looking people, stood on it, and began speaking. I detected a wall of apathy. It was horrible. After fifteen minutes I stopped and suggested we go somewhere else. I wasn't too excited about the famous MacArthur Park.

A Long Way from Home

I asked if there was any other place where people gathered. My friend suggested Venice Beach. He was right. Plenty of people walked along the beachfront, giving an atmosphere similar to Speaker's Corner in the Square. After looking at some of the other speakers and different acts (jugglers, magicians, etc.), I put my box on the ground, stepped onto it, and began talking on the subject of atheism.

It's amazing what goes through your mind when you are speaking. Here I was in celebrated Los Angeles, seven thousand miles from my home country. In the three weeks we had been in the U.S., I hadn't really missed our country. The fact was, so much had been going on that I was too busy to miss it. I hadn't seen a New Zealander since we arrived, nor did I expect to, so far from home and in a city of over eight million people.

After the crowd gathered to listen, I tried to get some sort of reaction by asking if there were any atheists in the crowd. Only one person responded. The accent seemed familiar, so I asked, "Are you Australian?" The reply came, "No, New Zealander... *and you're a long way from the Square!*"

Over the next few weeks, I was kept busy doing other important things one has to do with such a change in lifestyle —obtaining a new driver's license, etc. Then it was time to find some listeners again. I didn't want to return to MacArthur Park, so I asked a friend who knew L.A. to take me around the downtown area and show me some of the other places where people gathered. As we drove past a park amid the high-risers, I distinctly felt God speak to my heart, "I have already told you where to preach." It was a still, small voice, but so clear.

Back to the Park

As I placed my soapbox on the ground at MacArthur Park, I knew that I was in need of three things. First, I needed encouragement to preach in that place. Second, I needed God's help when speaking—I had to break through the apathy. And third, I had to stay upwind from the restrooms.

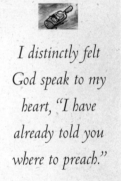

God gave me all three. When I handed out literature after speaking, every single tract was taken. I didn't get one refusal, which had never happened before. It was just a little thing, but it was all I needed to want to go back the next day.

I distinctly felt God speak to my heart, "I have already told you where to preach."

The following day, Sue came with me. As we walked in front of the lust-filled eyes of the park occupants, she clung to my arm in a way she never had before. She was scared, and I didn't blame her. I took her to the safety of a large store to do some shopping while I preached.

That day we brought some sandwiches that we had put together using hamburger buns. I wasn't sure if people would be insulted by our offer of "charity." They weren't. When they saw I had a box full of free food, I was besieged with requests.

After speaking to a small crowd of attentive listeners for about twenty minutes, I noticed a large goose making its way toward me. To my surprise, it began pecking at my sneaker. After thirty seconds of pecking, it moved to my lace and spent a good twenty seconds pulling at it until it was undone.

Fifteen seconds on the sock, then to my horror, it started pecking at my leg. I jumped off the soapbox and tried to scare the thing away. After some time, one of the locals shooed the bird away for me.

The next day, right in the middle of my message, I noticed the beast making its way toward me again. I refused to be distracted. He began pecking at my sneaker. I kept on preaching. One quick pull and the lace was undone, then right on to the sock. I looked down to see delight in his eyes: he could smell the main course. Suddenly he lunged at my flesh. I screamed and jumped off the box again. Then (God is my witness) *that bird jumped onto the soapbox...and wouldn't get off!* The crowd doubled in size.

By the way, if you have ever wondered where "Legion" went after he left the pigs (in Mark chapter 5), he went into the goose at MacArthur Park.

Preaching to the Choir

The following week was a trial. I found it very difficult to get listeners. I became so desperate, I began to look longingly for Legion. He must have grown bored in the goose and moved into massive flocks of pigeons, which on a number of occasions swooped in front of me as I was speaking. It was a little disconcerting as I had been "hit" by birds a few times while preaching in the past.

During that week, as I drove to the park, I prayed that God would cause me to look upon every soul as I would a precious jewel. When you pick up a valuable diamond, you don't throw it around lightly. Your knowledge of its value causes you to handle each one with individual care. That would be my attitude toward those who listened. Numbers didn't matter.

After speaking for a while, all my initial listeners left, except for two men sitting on a bench in front of me. I remembered my prayer and began seeing these two as being precious in the sight of God. I went through the Ten Commandments, explaining in depth what each one meant. I opened each commandment to reveal its truth in the light of New Testament teaching, explaining that God "requires truth in the inward parts," that He has set aside a day in which He will judge the world in righteousness. I climaxed with the cross and the love of God so evidently expressed in the death of Jesus Christ. Then I carefully went through the need for repentance. I put my body and soul into the message. At the conclusion, the gentleman on the right walked up to me and said, "Praise the Lord. I needed that," and walked off. I couldn't believe it. I had been "preaching to the choir"—in other words, wasting my time.

I looked across to my only remaining listener and whimpered, "Do you know the Lord?" He looked puzzled, shrugged his shoulders and replied, "No speaka English!"

The next few days were almost as discouraging. In fact, one day after preaching to five people, I sneaked across to Hollywood and preached on Hollywood Boulevard. The only place I could find to speak was at a wide portion of the sidewalk to a group of people waiting at a bus stop. Most seemed to be listening... until a bus stopped and stole my crowd. I ended up talking to one rather large jewel left alone on the seat. He was probably deaf.

That evening I switched on the car radio, disheartened. As I listened, something a pastor said grabbed my attention:

"God wants to raise up a testimony right in the midst of the worst Satan can dish out, and He wants to use *you*." It was all I needed to stay with my convictions.

The next day I went back to the park. This time I decided to go to an area I had been avoiding. A friend named Chris, who was visiting from Canada, gave me nothing but encouragement to stick with the preaching.

Chris accompanied me and brought his camera to take some pictures. As he walked through the park, a woman approached him and said, "What are you doing with that camera? I've been sent to tell you this is the Colombian cocaine connection. You go pointing that thing around here, *you're gonna end up in the lake,* and so is your camera!" At that point, we didn't realize what it meant to end up in the lake. Cocaine is big business in L.A. *Speculator Magazine* wrote, "In Los Angeles, cocaine dealers can buy a kilogram for about $12,000 and sell it in small packets for $250,000. A nine-year-old "runner" can be paid up to $100 a day, while a slightly older runner may make up to $300 a day." In May 1991, authorities in L.A. seized cocaine with a street value of over $500 *million.*

I moved even further into the darkest area of the park. I had found the pit of the park.

The lake at MacArthur Park was a very wet graveyard. The first day I spoke, I challenged the listeners to repent, saying I would baptize them in the lake. The next day I happened to look into it and see the condition of the water. To call it putrid would be praise. Total immersion would probably send the new convert to be with the Lord.

I moved even further into the darkest area of the park. The difference of a hundred yards was amazing. I had found the pit of the park. As I spoke, people milled around as though I didn't exist. There were blacks, a few Cubans, some Hispanics, and a scattering of whites. The place looked like an outdoor supermarket, without the hygiene and the groceries. People, pushing their entire worldly goods in supermarket carts, meandered around the area. Some had lived there for years. The police passed through in their cars, only rarely stopping to get out. I guess they had the good sense not to.

CHAPTER 6

WATCH YOUR BACK!

s I spoke in the pit of MacArthur Park, a pretty blonde girl called "Snow" sat down to listen. She even began heckling me. Her philosophy was that Jesus died on the cross for all humanity, so we could carry on as we are. As far as she was concerned, there was no need for any change.

To illustrate the fact that you must receive God's provision to partake of it, I got out my wallet and held up a dollar to give away. Suddenly there was a rush for the bill! Two wide-eyed men grabbed for it at the same time and tore it in two. I spoke for a minute on the fact that faith without works is dead and that it wasn't enough to merely *believe* in the money; they had to *receive* it. Then I reached down and picked up the bag of sandwiches I had brought to give away. There was another rush forward as hands by the score grasped for the food. Amid the noise and confusion, I heard a voice whisper, in a very sober tone, *"You should not have done that. Watch your back!"* It was Snow. In my naiveté, I had taken out my wallet, and was now a prime candidate for a knife in the back.

From that day on, I left my wallet at home, keeping my driver's license and other important cards in my sock. I also stopped giving away money. It caused too many problems.

It was so hard to sift through the lies and find a point where common sense and compassion met.

In the rush, bills were torn more than once. On one of those occasions, the guy who grabbed it first then ran around with a steel bar to rearrange the face of the guy who had ripped it out of his hand. He said that it wasn't the dollar, but the "principle of the thing."

I learned quickly that people there would do anything for a buck, even cultivate wounds so we would have sympathy and give them money to get to the hospital. Any cash given would more than likely be used for cocaine. Still, it was so hard to sift through the lies and find a point where common sense and compassion met.

One elderly man rolled up his pant leg to show me his wound. The lower leg, from just below the knee, was white and scaly, and there was a one-inch gouge in his flesh that was at least half an inch deep. The skin resembled meat you'd find in the trash bin after it had been there for two weeks; it looked ashen and lifeless. He said he didn't have any money to get to a hospital. I had deliberately left mine at home, so I obtained a few dollars from a friend and told the man that if he didn't use the money to get that wound tended to, I would be very mad. When others saw him take the money, I was immediately deluged with a display of swollen fingers, gashed legs, and stories about being unable to get to the hospital because of a lack of cash.

Four days later the elderly man approached me as I was getting up to speak. He had actually gone to the hospital, and they told him that he had gangrene and would more than likely lose the leg. He then looked at my bag of sandwiches and asked for one. I usually withheld the food until after I had spoken, holding a sandwich and speaking about the Bread of Life. However, this day I gave him one before I spoke. People quickly appeared from nowhere asking for food. One guy on crutches interrupted my preaching, saying that he couldn't listen while he was hungry. I threw him some food and kept on speaking.

Suddenly I was aware that someone was behind me. Since I had been told to watch my back, I stood with a tree directly behind me, but from behind it, I could see a hand reaching into my bag of sandwiches. It was the old man. I grabbed the bag and told him not to steal. Meanwhile the crowd was pressing in too close. I quickly finished my message, then before I could pass out the food, I was surrounded by hands reaching out, faces straining, eyes pleading. I could see the disappointment in the eyes of those who had missed out. I thought I'd brought enough food, but I hadn't. These people were *really* hungry.

After the crowd cleared, I continued speaking to those who would listen, then I went over to the old man and asked whether he would mind if I prayed that God would heal his leg. After praying I told him, "Don't steal. If you are hungry, tell me and I'll make sure you get two sandwiches." He was just about crying as he said, "I'm sorry, I'm sorry." There is something so sad and pitiful about another human being stealing one measly sandwich. I was told by a regular that the sandwich would be the only "meal" they would get that day. I controlled my emotions until I got home, then broke down in tears while telling Sue.

There are those who would say that giving these people food is wrong because most of them are using drugs. They would say that in one sense, it's just feeding their habit. But I have no problem with that because I am commanded to love my neighbor as myself, regardless of what he does with my love. I know that the Bible says to feed the hungry and clothe the naked. I know that I am even told to feed my *enemy* and to *do good to those who despitefully use me.* I'm prepared to give food not only to alcoholics and drug addicts, but to adulterers, fornicators, and even the self-righteous, if they are hungry. Some people seem to miss the spirit of Christianity. The essence of our faith is seen in 1 Corinthians 5:10, where it says that we are to be friends with the sexually immoral, the covetous, extortionists, and idolaters. The only people we are to avoid, according to verse 11, are the hypocrites. I would love some church to shock the world by putting a sign in front of their building that says: "Abortionists, rapists, murderers, drug addicts, alcoholics, adulterers, fornicators, thieves, liars, and even the self-righteous are welcome here—for such were some of us. Hypocrites, please go somewhere else."

Look at God's expressed will for us, so clearly given in Isaiah 58:6,7: "Is this not the fast that I have chosen: To loose the bands of wickedness, to undo the heavy burdens, to let the oppressed go free, and that you break every yoke? Is it not to share your bread with the hungry, and that you bring to your house the poor who are cast out; when you see the naked, that you cover him, and not hide yourself from your own flesh?" We are called primarily to "seek and save that which was lost," to set the captives free (with the help of God), to let the light of the gospel dispel the power of death in the lives of those who sit in its dark shadow. Then, from our faith should issue the fruits of good works, one of which should be to take care of the poor and destitute.

Corn Flake Handshake

One thing I became familiar with at MacArthur Park was something we called the "corn flake" handshake. After one of the team got scabies, we usually put on rubber gloves before we gave out food, for AIDS protection more than anything.

Many times after I'd removed the gloves, someone would approach me and say, "I really appreciate what you are doing for us," and extend his grateful hand. The first park handshake I received made me wonder, *What's he doing with corn flakes in the palm of his hand?* (The "corn flake" handshake is one where there are unidentifiable "encrustations" on the palm of the hand.)

I was slowly being stripped of my naiveté. I took Chuck, a friend, to the park, and because he had been raised on the street, he immediately spotted a cop in an unmarked car as soon as we pulled up. He could tell it was a police officer waiting for a drug bust because he was parked in a red zone, his license plate began with an "E," and there was a number below the trunk, meaning it was a government-issued car.

As I spoke that day, two tall, well-dressed men listened to my every word, and even quoted some of the Scriptures as I preached them. When I distributed the food, one of the guys missed out. I had, in the rush, placed the sandwich into the grasping hand next to his. His eyes flashed with anger. My friend told me afterward that he couldn't believe I had not given him one. He asked, "Didn't you see the knife he had strapped to his leg?"

The reason they were standing so close was to check me out, to see if I was there to deal on their turf. Chuck told me that a dealer is easy to spot. He wears jewelry, smooth clothes, and expensive sneakers. These two were dealers. Chuck also noticed five drug deals, just during the time I was speaking. I didn't see even one. Another friend, who had waited a short time for me to arrive, was propositioned three times by drug dealers and twice by homosexuals, both of whom asked him, "How much?"

A few days later while I was giving out sandwiches, I told the crowd not to take more than one. If they had received a sandwich, they were to ease off and let others take one. If they took two, they would be depriving others of food. Standing behind me I noticed a heavy-looking man reaching out his hand for a sandwich. I couldn't believe what I saw: tucked into his coat pocket was one I had just given him! I had told them that they were to have one each. I felt angry. Other people were hungry, and he wanted more. As far as I was concerned, this was the height of deceit, and there was no way he was going to get another one. So I turned to him, pointed to the sandwich and bluntly asked, "What's that in your pocket?" He snapped back, "A knife!" to which I politely replied, "Here, have another sandwich."

Shouting Sheep

It was an interesting morning; someone had left 120 sandwiches and two dozen loaves of bread on our doorstep. I was so pleased. I couldn't help thinking of the billions of dollars tied up in the buildings less than a mile from the park (one bank even had real gold decorations on the front of it), yet just down the road people were crying because they were so hungry. From that day on, the women in our church made sandwiches each day.

The week was a memorable one. At its beginning, some-one had been stabbed during the night and his body had been thrown into the lake. That day I preached and then asked if anyone wanted to become a Christian. I did so after elimi-nating every motive I could think of that would produce false conversions. I explained that the promise of Scripture to those who would come to Christ was not one of happi-ness, but of trials. I stressed the fact that those who put their faith in Jesus would be hated for His name's sake. I added that the bonus on top of the trials was the unspeakable gift of eternal life.

I explained that God considered lust to be the same as adultery, and hatred the same as murder. Then I concluded, "So you understand that God is angry because of your sin, that Jesus died on the cross to take the punishment for you. He paid the fine so that you could walk free from the court-room, and today if you want to repent and yield your life to God, come right now and stand on my left." Three men and a woman immediately responded. I prayed with them, gave each a Bible and a booklet, then handed out the sandwiches.

The next day, another group of people responded to the call to repentance. It was strange. I had been sowing for so long that when God let me reap I could hardly believe it.

Before we left New Zealand, I had spoken in two church-es on one Sunday morning. I mistakenly double-booked the engagements and had to rush from one assembly to another. After I left the first church, there was a "move of God." Peo-ple broke down and wept. I was hoping that the same would happen after I left the country. Now God was letting me reap in the land we had made our new home.

The following day, I was almost crushed by the crowd pushing forward for sandwiches. It was getting out of con-trol. People were yelling that others were nothing but animals, and they sure seemed to act like it. I tried all sorts of things to bring order. I drew a line on the ground and told them not to cross it. That didn't work. I told them to line up. That had no effect either. I once took along bags of potato chips and assured them that there was enough for everyone. The message seemed to get through and the line stayed orderly. However, others began arriving and, instead of going to the back, they went to the front. Suddenly we had a bottleneck in the front of the line and angry people at the back of the line. Then, like a shaken bottle of soda, the hungry people at the back burst through the bottleneck. They all came forward with such force, trampling the bags of chips, that I could hear them bursting (the bags, that is).

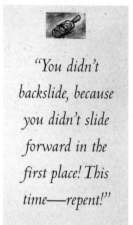

"You didn't backslide, because you didn't slide forward in the first place! This time—repent!"

On the way home, I began thinking about what Jesus did when He fed the multitudes with five loaves and two fish. The Bible says that He spoke to five thousand men, and that figure didn't include the women and children. There were probably ten to fifteen thousand people who would have been *really* hungry, because they had followed Him for three days and the food had run out. If Jesus had multiplied the bread and the fish and called for them to come and get it, He may not have made it to the cross! There would have been a pandemonium that would have made my problem look like an orderly garden party.

So, how did the Son of God handle the situation? He had His disciples divide the crowd into groups of fifty. He then sat them down on the green grass. I had never understood why He did that until that moment. So that's what I would do. I would tell my somewhat smaller crowd to divide into groups.

It didn't work. Have you ever tried to break one hungry group of rebels into two? I can understand why the Bible likens us to sheep. I ended up with two flocks of pushing, shouting, shoving sheep. *Both* rushed forward as soon as I began giving out food. It then dawned on me why Jesus surrounded Himself with disciples. That's what I lacked: I needed help. I needed a few trustworthy volunteers from the crowd —which, I discovered, were as hard to find as hen's teeth.

Be Careful!

The following day, a man met me as I was walking into the park. He was friendly and very polite, and he shook my hand and introduced himself. He said his name was "Preacher." As I spoke, one very haggard, red-eyed female in her mid-twenties whispered, "Be careful. *I mean it!*" I wondered what she was talking about.

After I had spoken, Preacher suddenly appeared and began helping me give out the sandwiches. He seemed to be able to sway the crowd with a little more authority than I had. Was this to be my trustworthy helper?

I talked to Preacher afterward and learned that he was called that name because he had a Christian background. Since he had fallen away from his faith, I very firmly said, "Something was wrong, though, because you put your hand to the plow and went back." I continued, "You didn't backslide, because you didn't slide forward in the first place! Do it again, and this time do it properly—repent!"

I left him with those few heavy thoughts and made my way back to the woman who had warned me to be careful. It turned out that someone had been stabbed a number of times that morning and had been taken to the hospital with little chance of survival. She was trying to warn me that the guy who had done the stabbing was still in the park. I asked her who had plunged the knife so many times into another person. It was the one who had stood beside me—my congenial helper, Preacher. From then on I decided to watch my side as well as my back.

The next day the place was deserted. I stood and looked at the empty benches. There were usually at least one or two sitting on the seats. As I pondered the situation, a voice interrupted my thoughts. It was that of a girl in her late teens. She was pretty, in a hard sort of way, until she opened her mouth. Her teeth were a jagged, blackened mess. She said, "Someone was shot to death here this morning—used to be my ol' man…" Then she said something so sexually obscene it made my ears tingle. I thought I was past being shocked, and managed to mumble something about not being into "that sort of thing." By now three or four others joined us. When I asked them about the murder, they said it was true, and pointed to the yellow police tape that was still in the park.

By this time, Miss Ear-tingler was crying as she talked about her ex–ol' man. Out of curiosity, I asked her who was involved. The reply was a quick, paranoid, "What do you wanna know for?" "No reason, just interested." The small crowd dispersed as quickly as it had gathered.

As I waited to preach, I mumbled, "Lord, I am not going to speak to no one. Please, give me at least one listener." Suddenly a woman in her early thirties appeared beside me. She was friendly, likable, and pregnant. I smiled, and in a non-interrogation fashion asked, "Did someone get murdered this morning?" This one didn't hold back. Her eyes grew wide as she pointed to where the shooting had occurred. She said, "When I heard the shots, I thought to myself, 'Stray bullets ain't got names on them,' so I hid behind a tree." She saw a man gripping his side, running a few feet, then falling to the ground...apparently dead. The shooting occurred in a fight over drugs.

I asked if she would be kind enough to listen to me speak. Most people fear speaking to vast crowds. That *used* to be my problem; now my biggest fear is the embarrassment of speaking to no one. Nothing feels or looks more foolish than a speaker who is speaking to nobody. She agreed to step back about twenty paces and just look as though she was listening. That day, I felt God's help. Most days I am aware of an "anointing," which usually comes in the form of clarity of thought and the knowledge that I am *really* getting through to the listeners. This day, it was particularly strong. I spoke on the subject of greed. I seemed to get more listeners when I said that the rich should share their wealth with the poor. I think they agreed with my thought that if God blesses a man with ten million dollars, he should spend some of that money on food for the hungry.

Then I asked how much they would give away if they were rich. I asked them to think on it. How much would we give away to help others? I could see that those who were listening were searching their hearts and finding what I found in my unregenerate nature—selfishness.

Afterward, my newfound pregnant friend came forward and said that she wanted to get right with God. She gripped my hand tightly as we prayed and she yielded her life to the Savior. I never saw her again. That was a good sign. Most times when I have prayed with people in a prayer of repentance, it was a good sign to see them come back. Not so in MacArthur Park. It was a good thing for people to keep out of that pit of temptation.

CHAPTER 7

LYING *in* *the* DIRT

I thank God for His Law. Without it I would feel helpless preaching to those in the drug world. To open up God's holy standard, the Ten Commandments, is to give them a glimpse of the Day of Judgment. It will be the standard by which God will judge the world (Romans 2:12). Without the Law, we have no knowledge of sin (Romans 7:7).

I have great confidence in the fact that God has given light to every man (John 1:9). No one is born ignorant about what is right or wrong. However, the more we sin, the duller that light gets, until it leaves us in the darkness of a deadened conscience. The Law resurrects a dead conscience.

I once heard a story about a man who was out hunting when a downpour began. He found his way to the shelter of a dark cave. Inside were dry leaves, some of which he made into a bed; the rest he used to light a fire. He then relaxed in his cozy bed of leaves. As the firelight illuminated the inside of the cave, to his horror, he began to see pairs of eyes staring at him in the semi-darkness. The light revealed to him that the cave was infested with rats, bats, deadly snakes, and poisonous spiders. He got very wet that day.

He who steps into the cave of sin does find a cozy refuge in his bed of dry leaves. But as the Law begins to bring light into his darkened soul, he slowly perceives his state in its true light. The penetrating eyes of lust and the horrors of sin are seen for what they are. A great preacher once said, "Sin then dwells in us, and not in the Law; for the cause of it is the depraved lust of our flesh, and we come to know it by the knowledge of God's righteousness, which is revealed to us in the Law...Without the Law we are either too dull of apprehension to discern our depravity or that we are made wholly insensible through self-flattery."

I was once standing in an airport in Oklahoma when I struck up a conversation with a woman holding a newborn. I remarked about how quiet her child was. When she told me that it would probably scream as soon as she entered the plane, I smiled and said, "I will sit as far away from you both as I can." You guessed it. When I boarded the plane, I found that my seat assignment was right next to hers.

After getting to know her a bit, I asked if she had a Christian background. She didn't, so I gently took her through the Ten Commandments so she could recognize her sin against God. Then I explained the extreme expense God went to so that we could be forgiven, which was to allow the death of His Son on the cross. I shared about the sufferings of the Messiah as He poured out His soul to death, that it demonstrated how serious sin is to God. Then I asked, "Are you ready to become a Christian?" to which she replied, "Yes, now that I feel guilty..." Guilt is the prerequisite to God's forgiveness. The Law gave her light. She was looking into the cave of her heart and seeing things as they were.

Every now and then I saw a resurrected conscience in MacArthur Park's dark cave. One day I opened the container of food and decided to stand back and let the crowd help themselves, trusting that each person would do as I had asked and take only two sandwiches.

Afterward, I saw that one man had *five* sandwiches in his hand. Right next to him was a very hungry-looking lady who had missed out in the rush. I prompted the man, "Why don't you give her one of yours?" He looked directly at her and said, "I wouldn't give her one if she was the last person on this earth." He walked off...then he turned around, came back, and gave her one. I was encouraged by that sparkle of light.

Candy Cravings

I have tried almost everything possible to draw a crowd, from mock funerals, which usually work, to having someone run around in a gorilla suit. I wasn't too excited about using these methods at the park. A Christian in a gorilla suit would be too vulnerable to attack, and I concluded that it wasn't a good idea for six men in white shirts, black ties, and sunglasses to stand in front of a corpse. They may look too much like federal agents, and we would probably end up with seven corpses.

I did stumble onto one way of getting instant listeners among those who use drugs and alcohol. Someone had given me a large clear plastic container of candy along with a box of sandwiches. I didn't bother to take the candy to the park for some time as I thought no one would be interested. One day I took it along. As I stood up while holding the container, I had an immediate crowd. It was only afterward that I was told that those who use cocaine have a craving for sugar.

The first day I gave out candy with the sandwiches, I learned an important lesson. The man who holds a knife in one hand and says, "Excuse my tactics," gets served first.

Feeding Tom

Every day I would stop my car about half a mile from the park, and give a man named Tom some food. Every day he would sit in the same place on a seat on the sidewalk. The first time I saw him I could hardly believe that any person could look so downcast. His legs were stretched out, his body was slumped over, his head drooped, and his arms hung limp, touching the ground. His skin and clothes were filthy.

I would often wonder about his background. When I asked why he sat there day after day, he gave me a long, rambling answer. I didn't have a clue what he was talking about.

Every now and then I would pick up a word that revealed he must have had some sort of education, but his brain was definitely scrambled. He couldn't even tell me how long he had been sitting in the same spot. I figured, by the grease on the sidewalk around him, that it must have been at least three years. Was he Vietnam veteran, or the product of a bygone drug era? God only knows the details.

I was able to find out that he did confess his sins to God, so I prayed with him for a time and left.

Let the Captives Go

While walking toward the area where I normally spoke, I noticed the old man with the bad leg, lying on the ground. I had told him sometime earlier that I would bring medical supplies with me to dress his wound. I kept my word and brought a first-aid kit, along with John, a close friend of mine. We woke the man out of his stupor, gave him food, and told him that we would be back after I had preached.

Again people gathered when they saw the candy. While I was preaching, I spoke against the spiritual powers that held my listeners captive. That day, more people came forward to make a commitment. Then, when the crowd began to push forward, I instructed them to line up—and, amazingly, they did. In an orderly fashion, each person got into line and waited to be handed food. It seemed that the usual confusion was more than natural, it was spiritual and could be dealt with spiritually.

When we returned to the old man, we noticed that he hadn't moved. The food we had given him had been half-eaten and was squashed into his clothing on his chest. Again we woke him from his stupor. After learning that he was called "Pop," we rolled up his pant leg to see the state of the wound. It was filthy. Besides the main gash, there were three other wounds. After cleansing away the filth, John bandaged the leg. The old man hardly flinched, even when the raw flesh was touched. It was a bad sign. As we walked away, John said, "With his gangrene, if that leg isn't taken off soon… *he will die.*" I knew he was right.

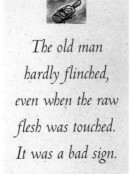

The old man hardly flinched, even when the raw flesh was touched. It was a bad sign.

We had to find a hospital that would take Pop. When we asked two policemen for advice, they recommended General Hospital. But the staff there said that, like all the other hospitals, they were so busy that they wouldn't keep him for long. From there John and I made our way to the Union Rescue Mission, which John said was run by committed Christians.

As we pulled up outside, my heart leapt with excitement. I spied a street-preacher's gold mine. There were 150 to 200 men waiting to be let into the mission. I grabbed as many gospel tracts as I could find and rushed into their midst. They took everything I had. Just as I was about to stand on a trash can and preach to them, someone called us inside. We related our story about Pop, and they agreed to give him a bed for the night. Then to my delight, they said that there was a chance I could come to the mission and preach to the men anytime I would like to arrange it. I wanted to stake a claim.

On our way back to pick up Pop, we passed some of the world's most exclusive and expensive hospitals. He, however, wouldn't be allowed to set foot inside their shiny doors. They were only for the rich. Money shouts.

The odds were, even at General Hospital, the old man wouldn't get his leg looked at for at least eight hours. He would have to just sit and wait, and there was no promise of real help.

When we returned to the park, Pop was lying in the dirt about forty feet from where we had left him. As we tried to rouse him, a few other park residents began to crowd around.

To my surprise they seemed to show real concern for the old man. They had never seen him lying around for so long. We asked him if he would like to go to a hospital. His answer was slurred, but firm: there was no way he was going. For about ten minutes we pleaded with him, trying everything we could think of, including telling him that he would die if he didn't get up.

Even with his friends trying to lift him up from the dirt, he would not budge. It seemed that we couldn't help him. There was no use calling paramedics, as they would only take park residents to the hospital if they were thirty minutes from death. In the end, as much as we hated to, we had to leave the old man in the dirt.

I couldn't help but see that Pop was just like the world. We were only too willing to carry him to the hospital and stick with him while that poisonous leg was removed. We didn't want him to die…but all we could do was to plead for him to change his mind.

The world lies in the filth of its corruption. It's easier to lie in that state than to make the effort to repent. But time will cause the gangrene of sin to spread throughout the body and drag the sinner to death and hell. Sin is so serious in the eyes of God, and the consequences so fearful, that Jesus said it was better to lose a limb than for the whole body to be cast into hell.

We would gladly carry those who would come to the Savior. He alone can cut away the poison of sin and save the soul. If any man is saved, he is saved by the will of God, because God is not willing that any perish. If any man perishes, he perishes by his own will, because the Bible says that "whoever" calls on the name of the Lord will be saved.

Pants for Pop

The day after we left Pop, I couldn't make it to the park. I felt sick at the thought of him lying in the dirt. In fact, I didn't get back there for another three days because I had a series of meetings in another state.

When I finally returned, the first thing I did was to look for him. My eyes scanned the park, but he was nowhere to be seen. Perhaps he was dead! I asked a few locals, "Where's Pop, the old man with the bad leg?" I was pointed in the direction of a body under a blanket. As I ran up to it, I saw that the body was completely covered, as is done when someone dies. I nervously pulled back the blanket and found Pop. Then I heard a wonderful sound. *Dead men don't snore!* I was so pleased.

The day we bathed his leg, I was disturbed by the condition of his pants. They were split, and since he wasn't wearing underwear, he may as well not have been wearing any-thing. So this day I brought him a nice pair of Levi's and a leather belt, as well as two thermal blankets to keep him warm at night.

When he woke up, he just groaned. I told him that I had blankets and pants for him, and said I would be back after I had spoken.

I placed the bag containing the clothes beside the box of food, stood up on the box, and began the message. After I prayed with those who wanted to commit their lives to Christ, the crowd moved forward for food. At that point I realized that I had forgotten to pray against the demonic spirits.

It was a good lesson. I grabbed one guy, moved him back a little, and told the rest to line up behind him. It worked for about thirty seconds. A dam of human hands burst onto me. I quickly pulled the large box of sandwiches back about six feet, and yelled at the people to regroup into a line. The dam burst a second time. I did the same thing again. This time when I stood up, I noticed the commotion had attracted two police cars. They came close, but stayed in their vehicles and watched.

Suddenly I looked back to where I had left the bag of clothes. It was gone. *These people had stolen from me while I was giving them food!* Most of them would steal their grand-ma's false teeth at the first sign of a yawn. I was so mad, I stopped giving out the food and yelled at the top of my voice, *"Who stole the old man's pants?!"* The police must have thought I was nuts.

CHAPTER 8

MORMON HEARTLAND

Although we had been in the United States for six months, few doors had opened for me to speak in churches. Yet Sue and I knew that we were where God wanted us. My first speaking invitation came from Youth With A Mission (YWAM), an interdenominational missionary organization. I had ministered with YWAM many times and was familiar with the way they worked. However, this invitation was a little different. Instead of teaching missionaries who were going to India or other parts of the unreached world, they wanted me to teach believers to share the gospel in Utah, the heart of Mormon country. Each year nearly 150,000 Mormons gathered in the small town of Manti, just south of Salt Lake City, to celebrate the history of the Latter Day Saints. After training, the believers would converge on the Manti Pageant to witness to the attendees.

I find it far easier to reason with atheists than with those involved in cults. Cult doctrines can inoculate sinners against the Commandments, making it very difficult for them to see sin in its true light. By their tradition cults "make the commandment of God of no effect,... teaching as doctrines the commandments of men" (Matthew 15:6,9). Yet because I trusted the YWAM leadership, I prayerfully accepted the invitation. I decided to take Rachel, my teenage daughter, with me, while Sue would stay home to take care of the boys.

Over the next three days, I shared some of the principles of evangelism I had learned in past years with the team that would go to the Manti Pageant. Many in our team had either come out of the cult or had loved ones still in it. They cared enough to want to reach out to Mormons who didn't know the Lord.

During those three days, I took the opportunity to read through a Book of Mormon, which was left in the hotel where we were staying. I wanted to learn some of what the Latter Day Saints believe, according to the teachings of their founder, Joseph Smith. Until then, I was very naïve about what Mormons believed. In fact, at one point I even thought, *What am I doing here—aren't we proselytizing?* I was in for a shock.

I didn't realize that the Book of Mormon was packed full of the words of Jesus and other Scriptures, with the words of Joseph Smith in between as extra "scriptures." Neither did I realize that Mormons believe in the "plurality of Gods," that God Himself was once like us, that God would have His power withdrawn if He did anything wrong, and that there is a "Mrs. God" (their God is married).

Nor did I know that they believe there was no virgin birth, that Jesus and Satan are brothers, and that Jesus was married at the wedding in Cana.

What confused me was the fact that Mormons, despite all this denial of Scripture, profess to believe in the Bible, specifically the King James Version.

After a Saturday night evangelism seminar, the team and I took to the streets of Salt Lake City to preach the gospel. One place where tourists gathered was directly outside the main gates of the Mormon Temple, so I organized pallbearers and a female corpse, put a sheet over her (simulating a funeral), stood on an overturned trash can for elevation, and began preaching.

With the help of a female open-air opera singer (who was trying to drown out my preaching) and another angry lady, our initial crowd of about eighty people nearly doubled in seconds.

Until then, I was very naïve about what Mormons believed. I was in for a shock.

I could see a number of policemen standing among the crowd, but fortunately they didn't stop me from preaching. The Mormon elders were overheard asking them if I could be stopped. When the police replied that it was my First Amendment right to speak, they suggested that I be arrested under the "Bizarre Behavior Act." The police declined the suggestion, saying the act was only for "flashers" and those who used the street as a restroom.

After arriving in Manti, we set up tents, prayed, and as evening came, made our way down to the pageant. Its site was ideal. A hill of green overlooked a field upon which were placed thousands of chairs. Above the hill towered the massive castle-like structure of the Manti Temple. The street bordered the area where we would preach and witness.

As I was about to get onto my soapbox to preach, one of

the older elders approached me and informed me that I could pass out literature, but I couldn't preach. Gently, I told him that I was going to. He then firmly told me that I wasn't. I cited the First Amendment, reminded him that this was America, and said, "I am going to lift up my voice as a little trumpet." And with the help of God, I did.

Buying a Gift

Within a few minutes, about four hundred teenagers swarmed around me. As I went through the Ten Commandments, they shouted abuse and became full of anger and hatred. I couldn't understand it. Here I was sharing what they professed to believe and they resisted it as much as, or even more than, most non-Christians. Out of courtesy, I stopped speaking before the pageant began, and spoke to individual Mormon kids. I found that many were into premarital sex, and yet they had total assurance that they were saved because they were Mormons. It seemed they preferred to embrace the teachings of Joseph Smith and their church rather than God's Word, which warned that fornicators would not inherit the kingdom of God.

Latter Day Saints are taught that there are three heavens. The first is the celestial heaven, where top Mormons go. To get into it, they say that one must add "works" to the grace of God. To them, Christ's death on the cross was insufficient. They are actually trying to pay for a gift, something that is not possible to do. If eternal life could be purchased, then Jesus need not have died. If we can *pay* for salvation, then it is no longer a gift, it is a purchase.

Those who don't "do" enough to get into the first heaven will make it to either the second heaven or, if they sin a bit, the third. So, who then needs to repent from fornication? It was obvious that we weren't trying to steal converts from another church, but from hell itself.

That same evening, I watched in unbelief as they mocked the cross in their pageant, singing a hymn about it in a spirit of ridicule.

A Touching Experience

The next evening the crowd was even more hateful. As I spoke, they threw anything they could lay their hands on. I read a few months earlier that two young preachers had been stoned to death by "fanatical Catholics" while preaching the gospel in Mexico. No doubt the murderers thought they were doing God a service as they hurled each rock.

That same spirit was in Manti that night. I was thanking God that there were no rocks present while I was speaking.

After I finished, I walked over to Rachel to see how she was doing. She felt the same as I did. There was murder in the air.

Within seconds, we were surrounded by about a dozen angry teenage girls. I tried to reason with them about why they were so angry, saying that I was only relating what Scripture says. Then I asked, "How many of you would like to hit me?" Immediately five or six hands went up. I decided that this was not a healthy atmosphere for my daughter, so I said, "Excuse me," took Rachel by the arm and began to leave that small crowd of girls.

As we stepped out of the circle of girls, I made an opening using the back of my hand. As I did so, I lightly touched the arm of the most verbal female. She spat out, "Don't you touch me...!"

Three minutes later, we walked back past that area and noticed that she was sobbing deeply.

Less than five minutes after the incident, a number of adults and the still sobbing female approached Rachel and me. One of them looked at me and said, "She says that you touched her *inappropriately.*" I couldn't believe what I heard, and firmly denied the allegation.

After they left, I began thinking of the word "inappropriately." It carried very strong sexual overtones. The more I thought about it, the more I began to see the seriousness of her claim. I was in the very heart of Mormon country, not exactly qualifying for the Mr. Popularity Award, being accused of sexual misconduct. My case wasn't very strong. There was the testimony of Miss Verbal and five or six eager witnesses who longed to do me harm. The only witness of my innocence was my own daughter.

I could also see the tabloid headlines: "Proselytizing Preacher Publicly Molests Mormon Maiden."

My imagination went wild. The prosecuting attorney would no doubt be Miss Verbal's Mormon uncle, and the judge, her daddy. Of course, the jury would be composed of committed Latter Day Saints and family members. I could also see the tabloid headlines: "Proselytizing Preacher Publicly Molests Mormon Maiden."

I began to imagine the shame of being deported back to my home country. The New Zealand media would have a field day. I decided to quickly leave the scene and return to the campsite before anyone got my name.

About an hour later, Lisa (another member of the team) and Rachel arrived and asked, "Have they come yet?" "They" were the police. Rachel then told me that the police questioned her *and took our names*. Things were warming up. We decided that it was time to pray. As we did so, I reiterated my assurance that God had called us to the U.S. and that no man could close the doors that He opened. We also prayed against Satan's power to discredit our ministry.

After we finished our time of prayer, another team member appeared and said that I hadn't touched the girl "inappropriately." It turned out that he had seen the whole thing and could testify to my innocence. We decided to go down to the local police station to try to clear my name.

Skulls and Guns

The prison bars looked cold, even from the outside. They were to our left. We turned right and followed a police officer to the police station's "counseling" room. It consisted of a table surrounded by six chairs. To one side was a glass cabinet containing a human skull as well as a mass of guns, steel bars, chains, and other weaponry.

I looked at the skull and asked, "Is that the last guy you counseled?" Fortunately, the officer had a sense of humor and smiled.

He took our names, dates of birth, and asked for our side of the story. We related every detail. He left the room briefly, then came back and stated soberly that the charge was one of "sexual assault." It looked like Miss Verbal and her lynch mob had already been to the station. *I didn't need to imagine any longer what could happen.* It was now a very real nightmare.

The officer left the room once again. A few minutes later he returned and said, "They filled out the complaint form, got to the bottom, then at the last minute decided not to sign it, and left. You are free to go. Do you want to press any charges?" The only charge I wanted to make was for the door.

After we left we realized that it was about the time we had prayed earlier that they had suddenly decided not to sign the complaint form. Thank God for His intervention!

At that point, I didn't ever want to see another Mormon. That night, Rachel was heard shouting in her sleep, "*Watch out, Dad!*" Good advice.

CHAPTER 9

THE POWER of DARKNESS

As I parked my car, I looked across the street at all the men lined up outside the mission. The sight was both exciting and pathetic. I was excited at the thought of speaking to them, but saddened by what I saw. These people were in the same category as those at the park. Some were sleeping in doorways, others were lying inside cardboard boxes. Small piles of ashes lay on the sidewalk, where some had burned whatever they could find to keep themselves warm at night, and there was the now familiar smell of urine.

I moved down the line, giving out our tracts. Most people took one, happy to have anything that would break the boredom of just lying around.

Earlier I had made an appointment with Alex, one of the administrators at the mission. I was told that he was the one who could give me permission to speak to the men. I walked

83

through the open doors into a large dining room where hundreds of men sat around tables, eating food that the mission freely gave them. I had a little time to spare before my appointment so I sat down to watch the hive of activity. As I looked at the faces in the room, I pondered the incredible creativity of the mind of our Creator. There are billions of us with different facial features, yet God has made each of us with one mouth, one nose, and two eyes. There were long faces, fat faces, wide eyes, squinting eyes, long hair, no hair. Some chewed with mouths open, others with more respect for onlookers. One man meandered around the tables still chewing on his food. He must have yawned and had his choppers swiped, because each time he chewed, it was as though his toothless bottom jaw touched his eyebrows.

He had no idea why he fell away from the faith, so I told him it was the old "moth" syndrome.

I turned to the guy seated next to me and asked him who paid for all the food. He replied that he had never thought much about it. I asked if any speakers preached to the men. After he answered, I asked if he had a Christian background. He turned out to be another of America's billion "backsliders." He said he had no idea why he fell away from the faith, so I told him it was the old "moth" syndrome. It seems that God created the moth for an illustration of a man's attitude toward sin. When the moth sees a flame, he loses what sanity he has in his tiny brain. He just can't keep away from the flame. Attracted by its warmth and light, he goes round and round in a frenzy of insanity, closer and closer, until he drops dead at its feet. Silly moth.

The light and warmth of sin so hypnotizes the sinner, he

loses what sanity his Creator has placed in his brain. In a drunken frenzy, he draws closer and closer, until death seizes upon him. Silly man. Jesus used harsher words to describe those who hear His sayings and don't do them. He calls them foolish. The Greek word is *moros,* from which we derive the word "moron."

I had to leave my newfound friend, so I told him that every time he saw a moth from that day on, he would think of what I had told him. Then I said, "Good-bye, Mr. Moth…" That made him smile. It was good to see him smile; it said something about his attitude toward me. Yet I longed to see more than a smile. I wanted to see those who didn't know the Lord come to recognize the insanity of their own fascination for sin's flickering flame.

As I waited in the hallway for the administrator, I was very prayerful. In a sense, I had to convince this man that I wasn't a wolf in sheep's clothing. I wanted him to trust me with his people, so when I spoke to him, I would have to blow my own humble trumpet.

After a few minutes, I was introduced to Alex and ushered into his office. I gave him an introductory letter along with two of my books and some tracts.

He looked them over carefully, then asked, "What sort of message do you preach?" I replied, "The Christian message." He smiled and said, "No, I mean, are you a *hell-fire* preacher?" I knew what he meant, but I needed to ensure that I answered his question correctly.

So I said, "I preach the Ten Commandments as God's standard of righteousness, opening them up as Jesus did in the Sermon on the Mount. I preach the justice of God, revealed in the cross. I tell people that God has set aside a day in which He will judge the world in righteousness, and that He requires all men to repent."

Mouthful though it was, he seemed to swallow what I had said. He lifted the phone and called someone, introducing me as one "who wanted to help at the mission." Then he set a date for me to speak to the men.

A Heckler at the Park

Thursday was medical day—the day John and I took a nurse into MacArthur Park to dress the wounds of those who needed it. Pop was sleeping on a bench for a change. I woke him and told him that we were going to bandage his leg. It took about five minutes for him to understand what I was talking about. Beth, our nurse, and Cathy, another young woman from our church, began bathing the wound. I was a little hesitant to take Cathy along to such a rough place, but after talking to her and hearing of her background, it seemed that she would be right in her element.

Dirty though it was, Pop's wound looked remarkably better. The green streak had disappeared. It seemed that God had answered our prayers.

After Pop's leg was treated, he really perked up. With tears streaming down his face, he admitted it had been giving him so much pain that he wanted to die. The pain was probably a good sign, indicating that there was life back in his flesh. He told us that he didn't have any idea how he got the wound.

While the small team saw to other wounds, I began speaking. I asked the people what they would do if they had a million dollars to spend. Each of us could live a life of luxury, right up until the day we died—if we had that much money. We could have endless pleasures, buying almost anything our heart desired, right up until the day we died. That was my point: *until the day we died.* Everything we hold so dear will one day be torn from our hands by the merciless jaws of death. The only thing that could ever really satisfy the longing of the human heart is to have death completely annulled from one's life. That is the precise promise of the Bible. When someone is born of God's Spirit, he doesn't receive a religion,[1] he receives the gift of eternal life. The crowd slowly grew as I spoke.

This day, I even had a heckler. I was delighted. A very self-confident man told me that he had never sinned. I asked him if he had ever lied. "Yes, but I've only told 'white' lies." I asked him if he "white" stole. After a little interrogation, this "sinless" man also admitted to stealing and lusting (which the Bible says is adultery of the heart). It was so refreshing to have a reaction from someone in the crowd. I deliberately baited him to speak out more. Suddenly he was gone as quickly as he had appeared. I found out later from John that two of the locals came alongside the man and warned, "You leave Ray alone... *or we'll cut you up!*"

As we were leaving, Pop came up to me clutching his replacement pair of jeans and said, "Thank you, sir."

I told him that my name was Ray, and that he wasn't to call me "sir."

"I will never call you Ray, but *sir.*"

"If you keep calling me sir, I will call you madam."

His eyes looked into mine and he said, "Thank you, Ray."

Christian Odor

As our team drove back, we talked about what each of us had seen. While the injuries were being bandaged, a man who was obviously blind made his way to the seat beside us. Some people look more blind than others. This man's eyes protruded and rolled independently of each other. John said that the whites of his eyes actually had hair growing out of them. He gently asked the man his name, then explained to him that Christians were bandaging the wounds of people in the park. The man asked if John was a Christian. As soon as John replied that he was, the blind man mumbled, "Well, I'm getting out of here!" and scrambled over the seat in a near panic. I was watching from a distance, ready to join John when he prayed for his healing. We were both disappointed at the man's attitude. He was a truly blind, blind man.

John's experience was a classic case of "CO"—Christian odor. The apostle Paul spoke of this in the Bible. He said that to those who love God, we are a fragrance of "life leading to life," but to others, we are an "aroma of death." We are officers of the Law among the lawless, and what criminal wants to hang around the law? The incident reminded me of a time when I was on a plane. When the woman seated next to me asked what I did for a living, I replied, "I write books." She was very impressed. With an air of excitement in her voice, she asked what sort of books I wrote. All I said was, "Christian." She then turned up her nose and said, "Ooooh, yuck!" Her reaction told me that I was sitting next to a big-time lawbreaker.

We are officers of the Law among the lawless, and what criminal wants to hang around the law?

John also related his observation of how many demonically controlled people he had seen at the park that day. He told me that they avoided the gospel like the plague. As I spoke he could see the powers of darkness steering them around me like some sort of magnetic field. He said that he had seen demonic possession while ministering in some places overseas, but that he had never seen it as prevalent as in MacArthur Park.

That day I had talked with a policeman who was escorting

a photographer so he could take pictures without any hindrance. I learned the officer was with the SID, a division of the Los Angeles Police Department that specializes in the investigation of drug traffickers. The Drug Enforcement Agency believes that street gangs in Los Angeles are second only to Columbia in supplying cocaine for the U.S.

Too Close for Comfort

On another occasion, John and I parked on 7th Street near the edge of MacArthur Park. As John was praying for our time that day, I was wondering if a drug dealer would approach us while we were parked. When I had pulled into the same spot earlier, a dealer had approached me before I even stopped the car. I remember feeling a little angry that a stranger would approach me so boldly. His face had the expression of a "time is money" salesman as he tapped eagerly on the passenger-side window of my car. In broken English he asked, "Do you want cocaine?"

The night before, I heard on the news that cocaine was now selling at a low $5 to $10, to entice school kids to become interested in the drug, so I asked, "How much?" Sure enough, the cost was only $10. Curiosity got the better of me; I shouldn't have asked. If the dealer had been an undercover cop, that question could have gotten me arrested. I found out later that the place was crawling with undercover police. Also, across the street, police with binoculars were watching our every move from high-rise buildings.

After John finished praying, we carried the food, drink, and medical supplies across the park, and I began to speak. I decided to see if I could provoke a response, so I mentioned that the reason the park was such a mess was that the people were too lazy to walk to the trash bins, and that they had lost respect for their environment.

That touched a raw nerve in one young man. He raised his voice in anger and yelled, "Who gave you the right to say that?" He was really upset, but I trusted that he would limit himself to verbal abuse because I had done him a favor a few weeks earlier.

His name was Kelly, a cocaine addict who most doctors would say had a bad case of schizophrenia. But it was apparent to us that his problem was more spiritual than natural.

When I calmed Kelly down, I tried to reason with him, saying that the park typified the lives of those who lived in it. They abused their bodies with drugs and alcohol because they had lost respect for themselves. If you have self-respect you don't pump drugs into your body.

After I finished speaking, we gave out the food and drink and announced that we would tend to any wounds they had. For some reason it usually took a while for people to come forward for treatment.

Our first case was a thumb that had been slashed in a knife fight over drugs. It had been left for eleven days without treatment and was badly swollen and infected.

I began talking with a man who had obviously been involved in numerous skirmishes. His right ear had been completely severed and his nose sported a scar along its entire length. He explained that, in a fight over watches, his opponent pulled out a knife and cut off his ear. He then casually pulled down the neck of his shirt to reveal a five-inch scar where his throat had been cut in the same fight.

I could hear John trying to witness in broken Spanish to the man whose thumb he had bandaged, so I thought I'd hand him a tract. One of our tracts had been dropped on the ground so I leaned forward to pick it up. My action coincided with a man walking past at that particular moment. He thought I was attacking him, and quickly turned toward me with a paranoid expression and clenched fist. I didn't want to be John's next patient, so I quickly managed a peacemaker smile.

Meanwhile, Kelly, the schizophrenic, was still raving in the background. He hadn't stopped talking since I stirred him up half an hour earlier. He paced back and forth like a trapped animal, yelling at anyone who even glanced sideways at him.

We were now washing deep stab wounds on the side of a youth's chest. The top wound was roughly stitched together, but the lower one was an inch and a half long and gaping open over half an inch wide. John explained that these types of wounds were very dangerous because if the lung is punctured, air penetrates the wound and creates life-threatening complications. I looked up for a minute and drifted deep into thought. Suddenly Kelly yelled at me from sixty feet away and snapped me out of it.

Mystified about what he was referring to, I called a questioning, "No?"

"Liar!" He screamed and rushed toward me yelling, "Yes, you did, *!@!#$. *You were looking straight at me!*"

His tone changed as he dropped to a lower gear, "I'm sorry, I blasphemed. I shouldn't have done that." Then he asked, "What would you do if I gave you this rock?" In his hand was a small off-white clump of cocaine. "Would you throw it into the lake?"

I said that I didn't know what I'd do with it.

"You throw it in the lake and you'd be made to go and get it back! If I gave it to you, would you give it back?"

Then he grabbed my hand and placed the cocaine in it. I grabbed his and gave it back, to which he snarled, "And you're supposed to be a Christian!" I wasn't quick enough to see that in the preceding five seconds, he had decided to reform his ways and give up cocaine... and I had given it back.

A giddy-eyed female grabbed the arm of her boyfriend and taunted Kelly, "And they say man can't live without a brain." The taunting seemed to enflame Kelly even more, so he began to threaten me with bodily harm. The lady and her rather large boyfriend stood up from their seats and came to my rescue. I didn't mind them interfering because, at four inches from my face, Kelly was a little too close for Comfort.

The taunting seemed to enflame Kelly even more, so he began to threaten me with bodily harm.

Then as quickly as he was stirred up, he was distracted by a prospective customer. A well-dressed gentleman walked up to him and began a typical park conversation:

"Got anything?"

"What do you want?"

"Whattaya got?"

"Anything you want. *Are you a cop?*"

The guy didn't answer; his expression of disgust spoke louder than words. A girl butted in, "He's okay."

While all this was going on—Kelly's ravings, drugs passing hands, and multiple stab wounds being dressed—some guy connected an electrical guitar to a cheap portable amplifier. The sound that came out was enough to bring tears to the eyes for the wrong reasons.

His music sounded like a cross between an untuned short-wave radio and a very sick dog. It seemed appropriate that he was singing what was probably an original song: "I've Got the VD Blues."

When the man first started "singing," Kelly commented that he wanted to go over and play some "praise songs." However, I was tempted to make a special request—that the man play "On a Hill Far Away." I was even willing to drive him there.

Bizarre Behavior

A couple of weeks later, as John and I once again walked toward the park, we could see a group of Hispanic Christians singing to a despondent crowd. The music was very Latin American, giving a festive mood. Yet no one was celebrating. There were no castanets, tambourines, or twirling females with flowers between their teeth. The heat, coupled with the general apathy of the crowd, produced a siesta atmosphere for those who could sleep through the music.

With the volume of noise, it was obvious that I wouldn't be able to speak that day, so we decided to go back to the car to get the food and give it out quietly on the side.

I wasn't too disappointed at not being able to preach, as we had just come from the Union Rescue Mission. Not only had they let me speak there earlier, but they invited me back to speak to the four hundred or so men in the chapel, in two different sessions. I poured my heart out both times and was fairly exhausted.

As we arrived back at the park laden with food, I saw Kelly. Although it had only been about two weeks since I had last seen him, it was obvious that he was wasting away. He looked like he hadn't eaten for a month. His paranoid eyes darted back and forth as we began handing out the food.

When I spoke to him, he didn't even acknowledge my existence. He snatched at the food and began ripping at it with his teeth, like a ravenous wild dog. Kelly was usually mean, but I had never seen him like he was that day.

A man tried to sell us six large cartons of milk, but when we didn't want to buy them, he kindly donated them to us. Then he pointed to the sky indicating that it was God's provision. It wasn't until later that I realized it must have been "hot" milk.

Although Kelly had received a number of free drinks, he grabbed a full milk carton and ran off. Someone chased him, took it from his hands, and returned the now twice hot milk. Back he came for more food. Even when he had eaten enough to sink a battleship, he was still nasty.

As he held out his cup for a fourth drink, a hungry girl held out hers. I looked directly at him and said, "Kelly, I'm going to give the young lady hers first." In a flash of anger, he lashed out at her cup, trying to smash it, but in doing so broke his own then walked off.

As we gave out food, he would accuse us of being racist, asking sarcastically, "If my skin was black, could I have more?"

Finally, I identified the animal that kept coming to mind every time I looked at him. His actions were similar to those of a hyena, as it ripped at the carcass of a slain animal, running back and forth, flashing its teeth in a show of vicious defiance. Yet, I still felt like putting my arm around him and loving him, in an effort to pull him back from the blackness to which he had so deeply given himself.

CHAPTER 10

INVISIBLE REALMS

I was having a tough time. I couldn't draw a crowd. In fact, I couldn't draw a thing. That's why I had photocopied a picture of John Wayne onto a large piece of paper and was coloring it in with paints. I couldn't figure it out. When my friends used a sketch board while speaking in public, at least a few people gathered. This day, no one bothered to give me a second look. I was planning to color in the picture and speak about how John Wayne lived and died as portrayed by Hollywood, and how he lived and died in *real* life. Death was no problem to the Duke; it was commonplace in the westerns in which he starred. So when it came to real life, one would think it wouldn't have bothered him too much. Naturally, it did. He called for Billy Graham to come to his bedside as he lay dying of cancer. The fact is, there's a *Hollywood* world, and then there's a *real* world. It is one thing to go out in a blaze of glory in a cowboy movie, but it's another thing to fade away under the merciless hand of a terminal disease. Anyway, there was no point in having a good illustration when there was no one to hear it.

Just as I was about to throw in the brush, a woman in her mid-twenties walked up to me. With an air of confidence she asked what I was doing with the paints and brush. I told her, and found out that her name was Jacqueline. I felt as though I had stepped into a John Wayne movie. She reminded me of the flashy-eyed female with a flower in her mouth and castanets in her hands, who twirls around the bar room, then jumps up and dances on a table amid the drooling of lust-filled, drunken cowboys. Jacqueline had no castanets or flower, but she had those same flashy eyes. As she spoke, I sensed that this sweet little kitten could, at the drop of a hat, turn into a ferocious wildcat. My first impression was an accurate one.

About two months later, I preached for about twenty minutes and was winding down. Thirty people had gathered to listen to the message and to wait for food. It was Friday, and the whole week had been a good one, with orderly lines for the food and quite a number of people making commitments to Christ.

Earlier in the week, my wife, Sue, had bravely come to the park to help me. I felt proud of her. Since she was 4'11", most of those who took sandwiches from her hands towered above her. She was able to get a firsthand glimpse of what I had been telling her about, seeing all those hungry hands grasping for food.

On this Friday, each person stood quietly behind the line I had drawn in the dirt about ten feet in front of me. As I spoke, I saw Jacqueline heading for me. I told her to stay behind the line. She took no notice, walked right up to me and demanded food. I told her to wait like everyone else, behind the line. She refused, and instead sat on the box I was standing on and hollered, "I feel like sex. I haven't had it for two days!"

I was annoyed because she had burst in just as I was about to challenge those listening to get right with God. The timing couldn't have been worse. I was also amazed at how her presence affected the men. Instead of continuing to stand orderly behind the line, they now pressed forward and were yelling and shoving one another. The atmosphere had suddenly changed.

She quickly grew bored and picked up a plastic bottle of water I had brought to bathe Pop's leg. Like the saloon girl with the proverbial whiskey, she took the lid off and began to guzzle it down. I saw Pop move to another location. As he left, I asked him to take the first-aid kit away so that it wouldn't be stolen. I told the crowd, which now numbered about fifty, that they wouldn't be fed if they didn't line up. No one moved back into a line. Other regulars, trying to be helpful, began to yell. Still no one moved. Even Preacher couldn't budge them.

The cowboy movie was still rolling. I was the local sheriff. I had the sandwiches under lock and key, and the lynch mob was there to bust them out of jail and gnash on them with their teeth.

A friend of Preacher's had a stick, and like a riot policeman began using it to push the crowd back. I jumped out of the way as they suddenly rushed the jailhouse. It was hard to see what was going on in the midst of that mass of bodies, but I could see someone lying across the top of the box, trying to stop the mob from busting up the jail. I could hardly believe this was all happening for the sake of a box of sandwiches! As I watched the fight for the food, I heard a bottle that someone had thrown smash behind me. I looked at Jacqueline, who was standing some distance away. She cringed as our eyes met. The little kitten had a twinge of conscience at the trouble she had caused.

A moment later, there she was, transformed into a wildcat, right in the middle of the men, screaming for food. She looked back at me and let out a string of hair-curling four-letter words. I made my way up to the empty box, turned to a guy who was holding on to six sandwiches and told him to give me one. As he did so, I passed it to Jacqueline, who snatched it from my hand and cursed me again.

I picked up the empty box and headed for Pop. As I did so, I saw that Jacqueline still had the bottle of water that I brought to cleanse Pop's leg. When I asked for it, she simply spat out more curses. I smiled because she reminded me of my regular hecklers back in New Zealand. Then I turned and walked away. As I did so, she called my name and threw the bottle at me.

Pop's leg was still a mess, but thankfully there was no sign of the gangrene returning. As I bathed the wound and applied a bandage, the little kitten came alongside. I told her to hold the bandage while I taped it up. She was a completely different person from the one who had so viciously poured curses on me a few minutes earlier. Afterward, without my asking, she helped me carry the empty box to my car.

Who's Pulling the Strings?

The first time I saw the television show "The Muppets," I couldn't understand how some of the puppets were manipulated. They were so well done, so realistic, that a small child could be forgiven for thinking that the puppets were real personalities in themselves. Those who are either babes in Christ, or are not yet born into the kingdom of God, could be forgiven for thinking that this day's happenings at the park were merely personalities enacting the play of daily life. However, those who are adults in the faith know better. Behind the actions of someone like Jacqueline, there is an unseen manipulator. She is just a blind puppet for spiritual powers.

Before I became a Christian, you would have had a hard time convincing me that there was a spiritual realm. If you had said, "Man is a spirit in a natural body," I would have been very skeptical. However, if you reasoned gently with me, saying that when someone dies the invisible spirit leaves the body, you may have been able to convince me of the fact.

Take for instance the doctor who says that a particular patient has just "passed away." You ask him, "What do you mean 'passed away'?" He tells you that the life has left the body. You inquire, "How do you know it left?" To which he replies that he didn't see it, but the invisible life-force, the spirit, left. What remains is a shell, commonly referred to as a corpse.

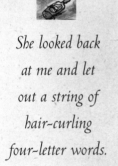

She looked back at me and let out a string of hair-curling four-letter words.

Many people find it difficult to believe in an invisible spiritual world, so let me relate it to a few things to make it more understandable. Think of an electrical current running from a battery to a remote-controlled car. We can't see the current, but we can see the car move as it is motivated by the invisible force. Or think of television waves. At this very moment, there are images of news reporters, cowboys, soap operas, etc., floating around us. We can't see them because they are invisible; they are in another realm. We need a television receiver to pick up the signal. The same is true with invisible radio waves.

For untold centuries, the hidden worlds of television and radio lay untapped. Two hundred years ago, the most progressive contemporary thinker couldn't have dreamed of what we have discovered hidden in the mysteries of the universe. Why then should it be so offensive to a reasoning mind to think that there are other invisible realms that haven't yet been discovered, realms such as the spiritual world?

Think of a man who has been involved in a terrible car accident, where both his arms and his legs have had to be removed. Literally half of his body has been taken from him, but he is still a whole personality. His soul is still complete. If man were merely flesh and not spirit, as some would have us believe, he would now be only half a personality.

Imagine if I were born blind. I'm standing on a street corner. You approach me, not knowing I am blind, and comment, "Nice day. It's good to see a blue sky."

I say, "I was born blind; could you tell me what *blue* looks like?"

You reply, "Sure, it's...it's...gree...no, it's...I'm sorry, blind man, I can't describe it to you. The only way you will understand the color is to experience it for yourself—*you need light.*"

The same applies spiritually. According to the Bible, non-Christians have their "understanding darkened, being alienated from the life of God through the ignorance that is in them, because of the blindness of their heart" (Ephesians 4:18, KJV). My earnest prayer is that those who have never experienced the spiritual birth are open-minded enough to receive the light of understanding from God, through these few thoughts.

Perhaps some have more insight than I had before my conversion. They may have looked into the occult and discovered that there is a spiritual realm. Or perhaps they have seen the incredible increase in satanic worship, accompanied by human sacrifices, cannibalism, etc., and know that this is a manifestation of a spiritual realm outside of accepted human behavior. Maybe they have read of people who are said to be "demon-possessed," or heard of serial murderers who claimed to be motivated by spirits.

I know what it's like to be Spirit-possessed because One possesses me. Since April 25, 1972, I have been possessed by the Holy Spirit. Every Christian is: "Now if anyone does not have the Spirit of Christ, he is not His" (Romans 8:9). But the Bible also speaks of another "spirit"—the "spirit who now works in the sons of disobedience" (Ephesians 2:2). Let's take a look at this spirit.

Hair-Raising Experiences

Allow me to share a couple of hair-raising experiences with you. Because I know that no liar will enter the kingdom of heaven, the following incidents, which are only two of a number of similar experiences, don't have even a tinge of half-truth or exaggeration. They are the "gospel truth," exactly as they happened.

While I was the speaker at a church youth camp, an eighteen-year-old named John stepped into my cabin late at night and told me he was having problems.

After talking with him for a while, I told him that we would pray about his troubles. As I began to pray, he slumped off the bunk on which he was sitting onto the floor.

Then he groaned, rolled onto his back, arched his body, and began pushing himself backward across the floor. Having the gift of perception, I realized that this wasn't normal behavior.

In the Book of Mark, Jesus said, "These signs will follow those who believe: In My name they will cast out demons," so I began to use the name of Jesus in what is called "exorcising prayer." The demons in John screamed, hissed, and manifested with such velocity that saliva from his mouth hit a chest of drawers eight or nine feet from where he lay.

With the help of God, I cast the spirit of rebellion from him, then asked a friend, who had come in to see what the noise was about, to get John a drink of water. When John came back to himself, I asked him what he had been involved in that got him into such a state. It turned out that he had been listening to occult-based heavy metal music *and drinking blood.* He and his girlfriend, under the influence of marijuana, would get a cup of blood from the local butcher and drink it in a satanic rite.

The essence of Satanism is rebellion. Those who give their wills over to occult influences will find a compelling urge to rebel against everything wholesome and good, against everything the kingdom of God stands for. That's why their ceremonies include blood-drinking rituals. God says that blood is sacred, so they desecrate it. God loves little children. That's why they have child sacrifices. God says the human body is to be covered. That's why their ceremonies are often conducted completely naked, etc.

The second incident happened after I had been preaching in the Square in New Zealand. Two girls approached me and said they wanted to talk about something personal. I asked if it was about demons. Surprised, they said that it was. One of the girls was having continual blackouts. For no apparent reason, she would black out at various times of the day. The blackouts became so frequent that the girls suspected something spiritual was involved. I told them to come to my office at 2 p.m. that afternoon. (This was while Sue and I were running the Drug Prevention Center in the Dome of the Regent Theater Building.)

The girls arrived at precisely 2 p.m. Frankly, I was surprised they showed up. I ushered them into my office and began to question the one with the problem. Besides the blackouts, she was having suicidal thoughts and, after some probing, I learned that she hated her father.[2] At that point someone came into the center, so I said I would pray for her after I served the customer.

As I stood at the counter, suddenly her friend burst from my office in tears and blurted that the young lady was writhing on the floor. The customer left rather quickly. I raced back to my office and found her crawling on her hands and knees, groaning, screaming, and making animal-like noises. Once again, my astute perception told me that this was not normal behavior for a young lady. I commanded the spirit to manifest and name itself, so that I would know how to pray.

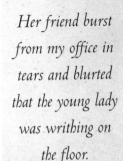

Her friend burst from my office in tears and blurted that the young lady was writhing on the floor.

"No, no!" it screamed.

I persisted. It shrieked, "Hate, Hate!"

I named the spirit of hate and commanded it to leave. (If you find this hard to believe, consider how I felt. You are only *reading* about it. I found myself right in the midst of something supernatural, illogical, and irrational, but I couldn't deny its reality.)

Another spirit identified itself as "Suicide."

I said, "Those are personalities—what is your *name?*"

"Soal," it screamed.

"How long have you been in this person?"

"Twelve years."

"How did you gain access?"

"Easily!"

During the manifestation, the spirits referred to the teenager as "her," that is, they were separate from her personality.

Finally, after I prayed for about an hour, she came to herself and seemed free. I told her (we will call her Jane) to become a Christian, or she would end up in a worse state than she had been.

I began to question Jane about her past. She told me that about twelve years ago, at the age of seven, she began talking with a "friend." This friend was invisible, but was very real to Jane—so real, in fact, that she asked her mother if he could come to dinner. He used to tell Jane stories. They were bad ones that started off good if she was in a good mood, and good ones if she was in a bad mood.

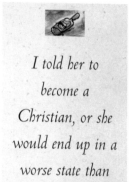

I told her to become a Christian, or she would end up in a worse state than she had been.

A few days later, I received a card from Jane, thanking me for praying with her. She said that she now felt free. On the card, she gave a reference for a Bible verse that she said meant a lot to her. We turned to it, and it didn't make sense as it was about the wrath of God. This remained a mystery until sometime later.

I advised her to get rid of everything that gave her contact with the occult. She was wearing occult bracelets, which we knew had some sort of demonic influence, and around her neck she wore a silver fairy, which I told her she should destroy. Unfortunately, as I found out later, Jane didn't heed my advice.

Two weeks later she called to say that she was experiencing more blackouts. I told her to come and see me right away.

Twenty minutes later her friend yelled for me from the top of the stairs leading to the center. Jane began to experience a demonic manifestation halfway up the stairs. When I got down to her, she was leaning against the wall, stiff and motionless. I managed to get her up another ten steps, but as soon as she turned the corner, she ran ahead and threw herself headlong over the balcony. I automatically ran after her, grabbed her and screamed for help. Two friends who were in the center rushed to assist me. I held Jane by her legs, while the rest of her dangled over the twenty-foot drop to the floor below. I knew that I had her life in my hands! I don't know how I hung on, as her body weight was over the point of balance, and with everything she had, she was trying to fall. We managed to pull her back and carried her to my office.

Horror Movie

As soon as we began to pray, Jane grasped her fairy necklace. She held it so tight that the blood drained out of her knuckles. It took me about thirty seconds to loosen it from her hand. I walked across to the other side of the office to an eight-inch-long piece of railway track that sat on my desk (at that time I was still making a few leather jackets for people, and I used the metal as a base to hammer domes onto jackets).

Jane was in a blackout state behind me. Two people stood between her and me. I had my back to her, so there was no way she could see what I was doing. I took the ornament and smashed it with a hammer. God is my witness—the second the hammer hit the necklace, the demons in her screamed. *I hit it five times, and each instant the hammer came down upon it, the spirits in her screamed in terror.* It was like something out of a horror movie! I picked the pieces up and threw them out the window to the ground five stories below.

Over the next few hours twelve spirits named themselves

and came out of her. The first one to leave called itself "Joseph Smith." Jane apparently had contact with Mormonism, and had even been baptized by them. The other spirits named themselves as Mocking, Lying, Deceit, Schizophrenia, False Tongues, Music, Affliction, Soal, Marinda, Strength, and Lucifer (which I would think was a lying spirit). The two that had the greatest stronghold were Strength and Marinda. I commanded, "Marinda, what is your function—what do you do?"

"I cause blackouts!" Jane had been having blackouts since her early teens.

During this time, Jane writhed across the floor, screaming, groaning, and choking. The spirits tried constantly to afflict her. On three occasions she grabbed lamp cords and tried to strangle herself. It took all the strength of four of us to hold her down.

She kept hitting her head against the wall or the floor, and she would pull her hands free and attempt to gouge her eyes out (I heard of one young man who actually did so recently, while being held in a police cell).

At one stage I noticed that she, in a total blackout state, put her hand down her blouse, pulled a safety pin off her clothing, and with incredible dexterity undid it with two fingers and attempted to swallow it.

As I ripped it from her fingers the spirit said, "I'm going to kill...." I replied that it couldn't harm us because we were Christians. It spat out, "Not you. *Her!*"

Jane lay in the corner in a blacked out state. Every time we prayed she would scream, and Strength would reveal itself by making her very strong. We found that if we named the spirit and commanded it to relax, it would obey our command. (Jesus said, "Do not rejoice in this, *that the spirits are subject to you,* but rather rejoice because your names are written in heaven"—Luke 10:20, emphasis added.)

For no apparent reason she began sucking her thumb like a baby. So I said, "Jane, I want you to answer, not Marinda. Marinda, you must stay relaxed—you must obey! Jane, tell me what happened to you when you were a baby."

She writhed in anguish. "They're taking me away from my mother. No, *no!*"

Jane, who was adopted, then spoke in a clear voice about her scarred childhood. She told us of her father who didn't love her. She talked about a séance at school, in which a spirit was manifest who said that Jane's friend would die in a car accident. The girl, aged twelve, was terrified. She became afraid to even get into a car. She was killed at the age of fourteen, when one struck her as she stood on the sidewalk. This left Jane completely filled with fear.

I always believed that hypnotism was delving into the spirit realm, but something happened during this time to confirm that fact. Even the snap of my fingers (as done by hypnotists) could either put her under or take her out of a blackout state.

She then spoke of different pains that she had suffered throughout her youth, including the physical pain of an ear operation. I asked her what significance her fairy necklace had. She said that it gave her a feeling of power over people, saying that as she held it, it caused her to "freak out."

I asked her about the card that she sent me. I said, "The Scripture reference that you gave me, in Psalm 58..."

Jane interrupted, "Not Psalm 58—Psalm 56:9."

We turned to it and read it aloud, "When I cry out to You, then my enemies will turn back; this I know, because God is for me."

The moment that Scripture was read, Marinda manifested with Jane screaming in terror. It became clear that Marinda and all her works needed to be renounced and turned from, by a conscious act of Jane's will. Jane then verbally renounced Marinda and everything associated with the demonic realm, and freely confessed that Jesus Christ came in the flesh (see 1 John 4:2,3).

The next day Jane came into the center and said she was totally set free—and this time she was. Although she was bruised, she didn't remember a thing after reaching that halfway point on the stairs.

CHAPTER 11

AN OMINOUS BLACK CLOUD

As I made my way along the aisle, I glanced at my plane ticket to ensure I was on the right flight. The airline had just changed its seating arrangements, and I was passing through the first-class section, heading for economy class.

As I did so, I looked at the extra room the rich are allowed. I noticed the full-length sheepskin seat coverings, the tables beside each seat, the free drinks, and the better food. Thoughts came to mind about the unjust system in which we live, where money has so much sway. It was obvious that this was nothing but class distinction. It was discriminatory. It made me sick.

Then I looked down at my ticket and saw that I had been placed in the first-class section. As I sat down on the soft, comfortable, genuine, full-length sheepskin covering, I smiled and said, "Wow, this is nice!"

The fact is, God has blessed most people in the United States with first-class travel. Yet it is so easy to let the good things God gives us crowd out the very thought that it is God who gives them to us. Most can understand that if I buy my children a gift, but they love the gift more than they love me (to a point where they shower all their affection upon it and ignore me), it is wrong.

When I look back at my childhood, I am amazed that I didn't see God's blessings around me. I was born just after the Second World War, and because my Jewish mother was afraid that another Hitler might raise his ugly head, my parents put "Methodist" on my birth certificate. In reality, I was given no instruction about God at all. During the twenty-two years of my non-Christian life, I ended up in a church building only three times. I found all three visits incredibly boring. The first time did have one highlight. I was staying overnight with a friend whose parents made him go to church every Sunday, so I went with him. The boredom breaker was the wine that was passed around during communion. It tends to hit the back of the throat of a ten-year-old and leave an impression.

When I was seven years old, an aunt taught me "The Lord's Prayer." That became a powerful sleeping pill. I couldn't go to sleep until I had rattled it off; I was addicted. But I could down that pill in nine seconds—from the "Our Father" to the "Amen."

When I was thirteen, Gideons International came to our school and gave each of us a New Testament. I didn't hollow it out to hide drugs in it as others did. Instead I took it home and read all of Psalms. That kept me busy for 150 nights, one psalm each night. However, that exercise did about as much for me as my three visits to church and the Lord's Prayer.

Around that time I remember hearing a converted alcoholic testify on a street corner about how he had had an experience with God. I thought it was nice that he had found help with his problem.

I hardly had any thoughts about God until I was eighteen years old. I was too busy to think of anything other than surfing. We lived opposite the beach, and I could see the surf from my bedroom. I spent all my free time there, and I even made a flag that was raised nightly by a well-trained mom when dinner was ready.

Dinner was late one Saturday night, so I decided to have a quick surf. I had a brand new surfboard and was still trying to break it in. I called my dog and headed for the beach. The animal was crazy, but went crazier whenever I mentioned the beach. He ran around in circles of joy. Chasing sea gulls meant as much to him as riding waves meant to me.

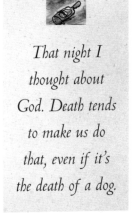

That night I thought about God. Death tends to make us do that, even if it's the death of a dog.

As we walked along the sidewalk, the joyous thought of chasing terrified gulls must have overtaken him. He ran ahead of me toward the beach. I called, "Jordie, come back!" No response. I called again as he ran across the road. Still no response. Suddenly, a car appeared from nowhere and struck the animal. He went underneath the vehicle and was thrust out the back. I was horrified. I dropped my new board on the sidewalk and ran out onto the road, picked up my beloved dog, ran home and sat at the end of our long driveway. Blood was dripping from his mouth and there was a hole in the unconscious animal's head. The car that had hit the dog stopped opposite the driveway. A distraught man got out, walked over to me, put one hand on my shoulder and burst into tears.

My older brother and I rushed the animal to the local veterinarian, where a day later they put him to sleep (the dog, that is). That night I thought about God. Death tends to make us do that, even if it's the death of a dog.

Three years later, in 1971, I watched my friends risk their lives by jumping off a fifty-foot cliff to kill boredom when there was no surf. One of them jumped first to see how deep the water was. He came up with a bloody nose, so from then on they jumped only when a wave rolled in. I refused to take a leap. I had gained an appreciation for life that was stronger than peer pressure.

Because of this appreciation, in October of that year I began to think deeply about the fact that one day life would end. Not only would my life end, but so would the lives of the ones I loved. It made no sense at all that everything I held dear to me was going to be ripped from my hands by something much greater than me—death. I was twenty-one years old, newly married, had my own house, my own car, and complete freedom to go where I wanted when I wanted. To say that I was happy was a gross understatement. However, I could see that my happiness bubble would one day be burst by the sharp pin of reality. It seemed an incredible enigma that the scientific and medical communities were preoccupied with things that didn't really matter. They were worried about space exploration and finding a cure for the common cold, when death like an ominous black cloud was looming over them. They were straining at a gnat while swallowing a camel.

Surely, scientific and medical researchers should focus their energies on solving the great dilemma of death. Didn't they have the thoughts I was having? Were they quite happy to yield loved ones to the grave without a battle, or at least a whimper of protest? It seemed no one talked openly about the subject. I kept such insane thoughts to myself.

I had been married for over a year. Sue had just given birth to a baby boy and I wept for joy at the miracle of childbirth. The happiness bubble kept growing. I was so thankful for life and all that I had been blessed with, but I had no idea *who* I should thank. The thought that God had anything to do with blessing was far from my thoughts, even when I rattled off the Lord's Prayer each night.

The Poison Arrow

I checked with Sue to make sure she didn't mind my going surfing with friends for a holiday weekend. That Friday afternoon, five of us left to drive 120 miles north of our city.

Early one night, I walked into Graham and Wayne's room. Wayne was already fast asleep, but Graham was quietly sitting on his bed, so I sat down to talk. During our conversation, the subject of God arose. Wayne woke from a deep sleep and heard us talking about God. He aired his disapproval, and was so offended that he left the room.

Graham and I spoke for six and a half hours that night. During that time I found myself confronted with the fact that I had violated the Ten Commandments. One Scripture sank like a sharp poison arrow into my heart: "You have heard that it was said to those of old, 'You shall not commit adultery.' But I say to you that whoever looks at a woman to lust for her has already committed adultery with her in his heart" (Matthew 5:27,28). It was the death of me. If God created my mind, He could see what He had made—He saw my thought-life. I was guilty of the sin of the heart a thousand times over. I knew that I would be condemned on Judgment Day and end up in hell.

I was trapped, a guilty criminal in the prison of Divine

Justice. Suddenly, the door began to open. Jesus Christ, God in human form, came to this earth and suffered and died in my place. He took the punishment due to me. He paid my fine. He alone had the keys to death and hell. For the first time in my life, the gospel made sense. I learned that the Bible says the whole of creation was subjected to futility and death because of sin. When Jesus came to this earth, He took the curse of sin upon Himself. That's why He wore the crown of thorns. That's why He died on the cross. Then He rose from the dead and defeated death. Graham told me that, if I would repent and trust in Jesus Christ, God would forgive my sins and give me the gift of everlasting life. Would I?!

I asked God to forgive me for violating His Commandments. I gladly embraced the Savior as a man dying of thirst grasps a cup of water. It was then that I found the God who gave me life.

The only way I can even begin to describe the experience is to point to a newborn baby. It cries the moment it is born. If I could ask what the problem was, the baby might say, "Something is missing. I don't know what it is, but there is an instinctive cry in me that won't let up until I find what it is." The doctor then picks up the screaming child and places him upon the mother's breast. The infant stops crying and suckles. I tap the baby on his tiny shoulder and ask, "How do you feel now?" He looks at me with tears of joy in his wide eyes, and says, "This is it! This was what I was looking for. I had no idea what it was because I had never experienced it before."

On April 25, 1972, I found what I had been looking for. I had no idea what it was until the moment I experienced it. The Bible says that Jesus Christ shall make you whole and "complete" (Colossians 2:10).

I went to bed at 3:30 that morning. As I drifted off to

sleep, I had a fear that what I had found would be gone when I awoke. It wasn't. In fact, it was so real, for the first time in ten years I didn't want to go surfing! I was quite happy to sit and read the Bible. That was very strange. It was in the Bible that I read about what had happened to me. The incredible peace I felt was what the Bible referred to as "the peace of God, which surpasses all understanding" (Philippians 4:7). I didn't just feel peace, I felt like a new person. My eyes fastened on 2 Corinthians 5:17: "If anyone is in Christ, he is a new creation; old things have passed away; behold, all things have become new." The Bible seemed to come alive as I read its words.

We told Brian, another surfing buddy who was with us, what had happened during the night. He was raised in a Baptist home, but he had never been born again as I had just been. He said that he desperately wanted whatever had happened to me, so that night we tried to duplicate my experience. We waited until it became dark, went into the same room, turned down the light, and prayed. Nothing seemed to happen. Brian was very disappointed. However, he simply had to have faith that, if his repentance was genuine, then his salvation was real.

The following day I went surfing. In fact, it was the best surf of my entire life. In ten years of surfing I hadn't seen such perfection...and I captured it on film. On reflection, it was a farewell gift.

Over the previous months I had been working on the production of a surf movie called *A Place of Our Own*. It wasn't a big production; I simply thought it would be of interest to local surfers. Using an 8 mm camera, I filmed all sorts of things that make up the average surf movie. Surfers have adventurous lives in that they are always looking for new surf spots. Some years earlier I had been the first to surf an amazing place named Magnet Bay. In 1965, four of us set out in an old Model A in search of new surf. We looked down on Magnet Bay from a three-thousand-foot hilltop and concluded that the surf was *very* small.

After driving down the mountain, through a farmer's field, around a gate, and over a hill, we were amazed beyond words by what we saw. The waves weren't small—they were perfectly shaped six-foot swells, curving around the bay. It was surf heaven. While the others raved and jumped around like excited kids, I put on a wet suit, paddled out, and caught a wave. Magnet Bay, plus other cool surf spots, is featured on the movie.

The moment I said the name "Jesus," half of the guys panicked and ran out of the

About a month after my conversion, I was still reeling at what had happened to me. I had truly been born again. I couldn't stop thinking about God and Jesus Christ. In the past, when I was on the phone, I would "doodle" by writing my name. After my conversion, with no forethought, I found myself writing the name of Jesus. I didn't understand it until I read in Scripture the words of Jesus, "When He, the Spirit of truth, has come,...He will glorify Me" (John 16:13,14).

Just before the premiere of *A Place of Our Own*, someone gave me a copy of *The Son Worshippers*, a documentary about the Jesus Revolution that was taking place in California. I gave myself a private screening on the wall of a spare room in my house. The producers had concluded the movie with one Bible verse: "And you shall know the truth, and the truth shall make you free" (John 8:32).

I stared at the verse. It seemed to jump out at me. At that moment I began to grasp what it was that I had been searching for before I became a Christian. It was *truth* that I was seeking. I was like a blind man groping for light. I had no idea why I was alive, what my purpose in life was, where I was going, or what death held for me. Now I knew the truth, and the truth had made me free. I couldn't wait to share this truth with others.

On the night I premiered *A Place of Our Own,* three hundred excited surfers packed the hall of the South Brighton Community Center. During the fifty-minute movie, I was very nervous because I knew what I had to do. After it was finished, I stood to my feet and said, "I now have another movie to show you. This one is better than the one you've just seen. It's on the Jesus Revolution in Southern California."

The moment I said the name "Jesus," half of the guys panicked and ran out of the hall. If I had cried "Fire!" they would not have left as quickly. My consolation was that a hundred and fifty did actually stay and watch the movie, and they remained in their seats while I shared with them how I had become a Christian. I told them that I had found something better than surfing. I had found the answer to death, in Jesus Christ.

CHAPTER 12

EVERLASTING GRATITUDE

The reason I preach the Ten Commandments is that I have seen the tragic result of preaching the modern gospel. As a new convert I ran around getting people to make "decisions" for Jesus, most of whom fell away. I would tell my buddies that I had found something better than surfing. They didn't believe that there could be any such thing, but with my continual hounding, a number decided to experiment and see if there was any validity to my claims. They didn't come to Christ because they knew they had sinned against God. Instead, they came to see if what I was saying was true. Almost all fell away from the faith, much to my dismay.

As the years went by, my itinerant ministry gave me access to church growth records. I was horrified to find that up to 90 percent of those who were making commitments to

Christ were falling away from the faith.[3]

One Friday afternoon, while I was assistant pastor, I was sitting in my office reading a portion of a sermon by Charles Spurgeon. I was fascinated to find that the "Prince of Preachers" used God's Law (the Commandments) to cause his hearers to tremble. This is what he said:

> There is a war between you and God's Law. The Ten Commandments are against you. The first comes forward and says, "Let him be cursed. For he denies Me. He has another god beside Me. His god is his belly and he yields his homage to his lust." All the Ten Commandments, like ten great cannons, are pointed at you today. For you have broken all of God's statutes and lived in daily neglect of all His commands. Soul, thou wilt find it a hard thing to go at war with the Law. When the Law came in peace, Sinai was altogether on a smoke and even Moses said, "I exceeding fear and quake!" What will you do when the Law of God comes in terror; when the trumpet of the archangel shall tear you from your grave; when the eyes of God shall burn their way into your guilty soul; when the great books shall be opened and all your sin and shame shall be punished ... Can you stand against an angry Law in that Day?

I remember thinking, "Wow...that's a little different from 'God loves you and has a wonderful plan for your life.'" I deposited the thought into my memory banks.

A few days later I was reading Galatians 3:24. However, instead of reading it as "the law was our schoolmaster to bring us to Christ," I subconsciously read it as "the law was a schoolmaster to bring *Israel* to Christ." The question suddenly struck me: Is it legitimate to use the Law (as Spurgeon did) as a schoolmaster to bring sinners to Christ, just as it brought Israel to Christ? It was such a revelation, it almost took my breath away. I closed my Bible and began to search for a sinner on whom I could experiment.

When I found a gentleman who was open to the gospel, I took him through the Ten Commandments first, and then I shared the cross. He stood to his feet and said, "I've never heard anyone put that so clearly in all my life." It was like a light went on in both of our heads. He understood the gospel, and I began to understand the great principle that the Law was a schoolmaster that brings the knowledge of sin, convincing a sinner of his need for the Savior.

I immediately began to search the literature of men like John Wesley, Spurgeon, Whitefield, Luther, and others whom God had used down through the ages, and found that each warned that if the Law wasn't used to prepare the way for the gospel, the Church would fill with false converts.

I began to pull together a sermon that I originally called "Evangelical Frustration" (later changed to "Hell's Best Kept Secret"). It began with the statistics that I had uncovered, then told the story of a youth who broke a speeding law and had no money to pay his fine.

When he was thrown into prison, his father arrived and told him that he had paid the fine for him. I *reasoned* that if the youth had been told the good news of his fine being paid *before* he understood that he had broken the law the good news would make no sense to him.

I could see that modern evangelism had made that mistake. It proclaimed the good news of the gospel (the fine being paid), *before* it convinced the sinner that he was a lawbreaker (that he had violated God's Law). It became clear to me why so many rejected the gospel in the first place—it made no sense to them. Also, because it neglected the use of the Law, modern evangelism substituted the promise of righteousness with a promise of happiness. Since the Law wasn't being used to *drive* sinners to the cross, they had to be *attracted* by the bait of "happiness." This wasn't only unbiblical, it was something that perverted the motive of those who came to the Savior. I was horrified at what I saw happening.

From the moment I became a Christian, I realized I had entered into a dimension that was totally foreign to the world of non-Christians. Therefore, I found that my language (of necessity) became pregnant with metaphors and analogies. I would say things such as, "It's like being blind, and suddenly seeing. You are like a man who is in a car that has a broken brake cable," etc. So it became natural for me to *think* in parables for my own understanding.

Friends called pretending to be Billy Graham, asking if I wanted to speak at a crusade.

What I saw happening in modern evangelism was like a man in an airplane being given a parachute with the promise that it would improve his flight. Over a period of days I thought through the analogy. If the man put on the parachute to improve his flight, then if he became unhappy with the flight (because of severe turbulence, for example), he would take the parachute off. But if his motive was that he had to jump, the turbulence would be irrelevant to him. In fact, it would make him cling tighter to the parachute because his very life depended on it. It was another breathtaking revelation to me.

I added those thoughts to the sermon. Then I added relevant Scriptures, and quotes from men like Spurgeon, Whitefield, Wesley, etc., about the use of the Law as a schoolmaster to bring sinners to Christ. Suddenly I had a complete teaching on the subject.

I began sharing "Evangelical Frustration" not only in New

Zealand, but also overseas. It was at a speaking engagement in Hawaii that Pastor Garry Ansdell heard the teaching and later invited us to base our ministry in the United States.

Things were relatively quiet for our first three years in the U.S., until I received a call from Bill Gothard in Chicago. I had heard of him when I was in New Zealand, but wasn't familiar with his voice. Friends knew that I felt frustrated as I waited for God to open doors, and they called pretending to be Billy Graham, asking if I wanted to speak at a crusade. So when a voice I had never heard said that he was Bill Gothard, I thought it was one of my friends kidding me, and for about 60 seconds I was waiting for a gap so I could say, "Yeah, and I'm Elvis. I'll see you at Disneyland." Fortunately, I didn't find a gap. Someone had given him a tape of my message "Hell's Best Kept Secret," which explains the use of the Law in evangelism. He was so impressed with the teaching that the following week he flew me to San Jose, California, and had me share it with a thousand pastors. He put the teaching on video, and in 1993 he screened it to 30,000 pastors. From then on doors began to open.

That same year David Wilkerson called. He had been listening to "Hell's Best Kept Secret" in his car, and called me on his car phone. This was a famous voice I was very familiar with. He immediately flew me three thousand miles, from Los Angeles to New York, to share the one-hour teaching with his church. He considered it to be *that* important. He even took me to lunch, which was such a thrill. As far as I was concerned, David Wilkerson was just one step down from John the Baptist. Come to think of it, I would prefer to share food with him rather than with John the Baptist...for obvious reasons.

To help explain the importance of using the Law in evangelism, allow me to share with you the complete parachute analogy. We'll look at the impact of a sinner's motive in his response to the gospel.

The Jump to Come

Two men are seated in a plane. The first is given a parachute and told to put it on, as it would improve his flight. He's a little skeptical at first, since he can't see how wearing a parachute in a plane could possibly improve his flight.

After some time, he decides to experiment and see if the claims are true. As he puts it on, he notices the weight of it upon his shoulders and he finds he has difficulty in sitting upright. However, he consoles himself with the fact that he was told the parachute would improve his flight. So he decides to give it a little time.

As he waits, he notices that some of the other passengers are laughing at him because he's wearing a parachute in a plane. He begins to feel somewhat humiliated. As they continue to laugh and point at him, he can stand it no longer. He sinks in his seat, unstraps the parachute, and throws it to the floor. Disillusionment and bitterness fill his heart, because as far as he was concerned he was told an outright lie.

The second man is given a parachute, *but listen to what he is told.* He's told to put it on because at any moment he'll be jumping 25,000 feet out of the plane. He gratefully puts the parachute on. He doesn't notice the weight of it upon his shoulders, nor that he can't sit upright. His mind is consumed with the thought of what would happen to him if he jumped without the parachute.

The Motive and the Result

Let's now analyze the *motive* and the *result* of each passenger's experience. The first man's motive for putting on the parachute was solely to improve his flight. The result of his experience was that he was humiliated by the passengers, disillusioned, and somewhat embittered against those who gave him the parachute. As far as he's concerned, it will be a long time before anyone gets one of those things on his back again.

The second man put on the parachute solely to escape the jump to come. And because of his knowledge of what would happen to him if he jumped without it, he has a deep-rooted joy and peace in his heart knowing that he's saved from sure death. This knowledge gives him the ability to withstand the mockery of the other passengers. His attitude toward those who gave him the parachute is one of heartfelt gratitude.

Listen to what the modern gospel says: "Put on the Lord Jesus Christ. He'll give you love, joy, peace, fulfillment, and lasting happiness." In other words, Jesus will improve your flight. The sinner responds, and in an experimental fashion puts on the Savior to see if the claims are true. And what does he get? The promised temptation, tribulation, and persecution—the other passengers mock him. So what does he do? He takes off the Lord Jesus Christ; he's offended for the Word's sake; he's disillusioned and somewhat embittered; and quite rightly so. He was promised peace, joy, love, and fulfillment, and all he got were trials and humiliation. His bitterness is directed toward those who gave him the so-called "good news." His latter end becomes worse than the first—he's another inoculated and bitter "backslider."

Instead of preaching that Jesus improves the flight, we should be warning the passengers that they have to jump out of a plane. That it's appointed for man to die once, and after this the judgment. When a sinner understands the horrific consequences of breaking the Law of God, he will flee to the Savior solely to escape the wrath that's to come. If we are true and faithful witnesses, that's what we will be preaching: that there is wrath to come—that "God commands all men everywhere to repent, *because* He has appointed a day on which He will judge the world in righteousness" (Acts 17:30, 31). The issue isn't one of happiness, but one of righteousness. The fact that the Bible (KJV) doesn't mention the word "happiness" even *once,* yet mentions "righteousness" 289 times, should make the issue clear.

It doesn't matter how happy a sinner is, or how much he is enjoying the pleasures of sin for a season; without the righteousness of Christ, he will perish on the day of wrath. The Bible says, "Riches do not profit in the day of wrath, but righteousness delivers from death" (Proverbs 11:4). Peace and joy are legitimate fruits of salvation, but it's not legitimate to use these *fruits* as a drawing card *for* salvation. If we do so, the sinner will respond with an impure motive, lacking repentance.

Can you remember why the *second* passenger had joy and peace in his heart? It was because he knew that the parachute was going to save him from sure death. In the same way, as believers, we have joy and peace in believing because we know that the righteousness of Christ is going to deliver us from the wrath that is to come.

With that thought in mind, let's take a close look at an incident aboard the plane. We have a brand new flight attendant. It's her first day, and she's carrying a tray of boiling hot coffee. She wants to leave an impression on the passengers and she certainly does! As she's walking down the aisle, she trips over someone's foot and slops the hot coffee all over the lap of our second passenger. What's his reaction as that boiling liquid hits his tender flesh? Does he say, "Man, that hurt!"? Yes, he does. But then does he rip the parachute from his shoulders, throw it to the floor, and say, "That stupid parachute!"? No; why should he? He didn't put the parachute on for a better flight. He put it on to save him from the jump to come. If anything, the hot coffee incident causes him to cling tighter to the parachute and even look forward to the jump.

If we have put on the Lord Jesus Christ for the right motive—to flee from the wrath to come—then when tribulation strikes, when the flight gets bumpy, we won't get angry at God, and we won't lose our joy and peace. Why should we? We didn't come to Christ for a better lifestyle, but to flee from the wrath to come.

If anything, tribulation drives the true believer closer to the Savior. Sadly, we have multitudes of professing Christians who lose their joy and peace when the flight gets bumpy. Why? Because they are the product of a man-centered gospel. They came lacking repentance, without which we cannot be saved.

How then do you convince a person that he needs the Savior? The same way you would convince someone that he needed to put on a parachute. You would simply tell him about the jump. You would reason with him about the foolishness of jumping 25,000 feet without a parachute. He must understand that there are terrible consequences when the law of gravity is violated. You would then let his natural reasoning do the rest.

The Delightful Frosting

A friend once purchased a very sharp bread knife, which was made of a steel that could cut through wood. It was *very* sharp. During a birthday party, the knife's blade was covered with frosting and sat beside a birthday cake on a bench. Suddenly Ken saw that his grandchild had reached up, taken hold of the knife, and was about to lick the frosting off the blade.

He grabbed the child and pulled the blade away as it was two inches from his mouth.

Sin looks sweet, but its cut is deadly. No doubt the child thought that his grandfather was mean for taking the knife from him, but Ken's motivation was one of love and genuine concern for the child's welfare. The tragedy with this world is that most of the sweet pleasures it seeks can be enjoyed legitimately. The frosting of sex is God-given. He is not a party-pooper when He forbids fornication and adultery. He merely wants to take from our hands the sharp and deadly blade of sin's terrible repercussion.

If we remove the Law from the gospel, we also remove from it the fierceness of God's wrath against sin.

The problem is that by removing the Law from our message, we remove the very instrument that convinces the sinner that his sinful delights are deadly, and he won't let go of sin until he is convinced of its repercussion.

If we remove the Law from the proclamation of the gospel, we also remove from it the fierceness of God's wrath against sin.[4] The natural progression is then to make hell's flames a metaphor and reduce it to a place of "eternal separation from God." Psalm 139:8 tells us, "If I ascend into heaven, You are there; if I make my bed in hell, behold, You are there." There is nowhere we can go to get away from His Spirit or flee from His presence, because God is omnipresent. That means He dwells everywhere. The concept of "eternal separation from God" (as a place of eternal punishment) is therefore unbiblical.

Many Scriptures warn about hell by describing it as a "place of torment" with "flames" and "everlasting fire," where there is "weeping and gnashing of teeth," and where "their worm does not die and the fire is not quenched." The ungodly "shall be tormented with fire and brimstone...and the smoke of their torment ascends forever and ever."

Every Christian who has a concern for the fate of the ungodly would no doubt love to be able to say that the fires of hell are indeed metaphoric. But if we say that the "fire" is metaphoric, then we must say that the "brimstone" mentioned in Revelation 21:8 is also metaphoric, which would make no sense at all: "But the cowardly, unbelieving, abominable, murderers, sexually immoral, sorcerers, idolaters, and all liars shall have their part in the lake which burns with fire and brimstone, which is the second death." Using unbiblical clichés such as "eternal separation from God," and presuming that the flames of hell are a metaphor, has tragic repercussions. It defuses evangelism of urgency and strips our prayers of passion.

Hitler's Morals

The Law of God is not only right and reasonable, it is "holy and just and good" (Romans 7:12). It is a warning to humanity of the standard by which God will "judge the world in righteousness."

I know plenty of individuals who consider themselves to be good people, but their standard of goodness is their own. Let's take an extreme. Adolf Hitler more than likely justified in his own mind his terrible crimes against the Jewish people. It is highly unlikely that he thought of himself as being evil, because (as the Bible points out), "All the ways of a man are pure in his own eyes" (Proverbs 16:2).

To prove my point, let me direct your thoughts to a recent survey of two hundred criminals in the United States. When they were questioned about whether they considered themselves to be evil, *not one admitted the fact.* It was reported that even while they were committing the crime, they didn't see what they were doing as an evil act. How could this be? Simply because he who steals, and he who is stolen from, have completely different attitudes toward the crime. One violates; the other is violated.

When King David committed adultery and murder, most would consider that his crimes were horizontal—committed against men. However, the Bible says that they were vertical—crimes against God Himself. David cried out to God, "Against You, You only, have I sinned, and done this evil in Your sight" (Psalm 51:4). When we sin, we violate the Law of God and so sin vertically.

We have a completely different attitude toward sin than God does. We find comfort in the sentiment "to thine own self be true," because many of us have been true to ourselves. The real question is, "Have we been true to God?" Have we kept His Law? To answer this question, we have to let go of our own standard and look objectively at God's standard. Until we do that, we will (like Hitler and the surveyed criminals) remain in a cloud of self-delusion.

Author A. W. Tozer said, "The vague and tenuous hope that God is too kind to punish the ungodly has become a deadly opiate for the consciences of millions."

A Well of Gratitude

Do you realize what the punishment is for breaking God's Law? Do you know that justice calls for retribution for every single sin committed? Jesus warned, "For every idle word men may speak, they will give account of it in the day of judgment" (Matthew 12:36).

Murder is a terrible crime, and those who take a life should be thoroughly punished by our court systems. Those who deny the existence of hell are saying that Almighty God, the Creator of the universe, has less sense of justice than man —that God hasn't the backbone, the guts, to punish murderers. Such a philosophy couldn't be further from the truth. The Bible warns hundreds of times that God has set aside a day in which He will judge the world in righteousness. He will not only punish murderers, but rapists, thieves, liars, the greedy, the lustful, the jealous, the proud, as well as all those who are disobedient to the inner light that God has given to every man. The day will come when every sinful deed, done in the open or in secret, will be presented as evidence of humanity's guilt in the courtroom of Eternal Justice.

Yet in His great kindness, God paid the penalty two thousand years ago on the cross of Calvary. His great love for the sinful human race was revealed to the world when God came to this earth in human form to suffer and die in our place. If we have true sorrow in our heart, guilty though we are, we may go free from the demands of Eternal Justice. The book was thrown at Jesus instead of us.

Those who are able to comprehend this incredible fact will feel a well of gratitude spring from the heart. They will, above all else, want to fall at the feet of Him who has shown such incredible love and unmerited kindness, and live for His will and honor.

It was this gratitude that helped me swallow my fears, step out of my comfort zone, and preach the gospel that first day in the Square back in my hometown. It was the same wellspring of everlasting gratitude that caused me to uproot my family, leave our home country, and—for the sake of the gospel—mix with murderers at MacArthur Park.

CHAPTER 13

IN *the* LINE *of* DUTY

I always enjoyed our times of fellowship when John came with me to the park. He was going through a rough time, as his father had been diagnosed with terminal cancer. The hospital sent him home to die, but through the power of prayer, God miraculously extended his dad's life. It had been a trying time for everyone concerned, yet through it all, John had been nothing but a source of encouragement to me when it came to speaking at the park.

Not only did he have a deep faith in God, but he had some knowledge of how to tend to those with wounds, something I sadly lacked.

Beth, our nurse, came with us once a week to help those who were sick. She was in her element. God created some people with a special ability to deal with wounds that would turn the most stable stomach. Beth had that gifting. We encountered injuries that had been neglected for months. One young man winced in pain as she pumped blue liquid into his mangled knee. The wound looked like an orange that had been split on one side and then turned inside out. Beth said afterward that she initially thought someone had put masses of ointment on it, but they hadn't—it was oozing with pus and other bodily fluids. His friends stood around and ate sandwiches as they watched her clean the leg.

A Different Name

As we were leaving that day, a well-built man in his late twenties hobbled over to us on crutches. I couldn't believe what I saw. This guy's ankle was in traction, and at three points on his foot, screws extended from steel bars through his skin and into his bones. At each point of entry, the skin was bulging with inflammation, so red and swollen with pus that it looked like it would burst. It turned out that this man, whose name was "Unique" (now there's a different name), had been sleeping on an eight-foot wall in the park when he fell off. The fall broke his ankle and pushed the bone through his flesh. He was put in traction, but instead of being confined to a hospital bed as is normally done, he found himself turned out on the streets. Now he was a sure candidate for having the leg amputated. It didn't matter how much we pleaded with him, like Pop, he wouldn't let us take him back to the hospital. He was terrified of the place. All we could do was wash down the leg with peroxide, tell him of his need to get right with God, and pray that God would heal him.

Sometimes even Beth was at a loss for how to treat some of the people. What do you do when a girl (who doesn't speak English) groans in pain, writhes back and forth as though she is continually in some sort of fit, and rubs her arms and legs, which are red, swollen, and rash-covered?

One day, while Beth and Rachel were seeing to a girl who had been hit on the head with a bottle (as someone tried to rape her), I was handed a small piece of paper. It was a spiritualist tract, encouraging the use of tarot cards, ESP, palmistry, etc. I couldn't help thinking it's a pity that the Church doesn't have as much zeal to go to the highways and byways as those who evangelize for the kingdom of darkness.

When I entered the park the following week by myself, I knew what I was in for. When I tried to give out food alone, I always had chaos. Unique was nowhere to be seen. Pop, however, was there, milling around those on the seats. It was a change to see him awake; perhaps he was sleepwalking. He was a different man now that his leg had healed. He was also one of the first to rummage through the box of clothes that I had brought to give away, despite the fact that it was full of women's clothing. He was like a greedy bargain hunter at a sale, pushing and yelling as he grabbed anything he could get his hands on. Pop's taste for clothes wasn't strange; he knew he could sell the articles and raise money for his cocaine habit.

I tried to save what I could from greedy hands, for the women who were pregnant. It was hard to believe that they were as far along as they were. The women were so malnourished that those who were in the latter stages of pregnancy were just beginning to show. Where I could, I would give them milk to build up their undernourished babies.

After the clothing was gone, I spoke about how Satan was destroying their lives. Ironically, many of them believe in a literal devil that came to steal, kill, and destroy. I explained that the Bible says they are in the "snare of the devil, having been taken captive by him to do his will," and that God is able to save to the uttermost, if they would repent.

I had seen a TV news item one night about an exhumation of a mass grave in Mexico. Members involved in a satanic cult selected people at random, then kidnapped, tortured, murdered, sacrificed, and cannibalized them. The horrific scene of the remains of at least a dozen people was enough to turn anyone's stomach. I remember thinking that I was glad to be far away from Mexico. Then the reporter stated that the religious cult, called "Santa Aria," wasn't confined to Mexico, but had a stronghold right in L.A.—in the MacArthur Park area.

However, I knew that the demons in the park couldn't keep people from coming to the Savior. In the Bible, a man who was possessed by multitudes of demons was still able to fall at the feet of the Son of God and worship Him.

Errol Flynn

When I finished my message, I said, "Today I have a big problem. As soon as I start giving out food, there is going to be a riot. I want some volunteer…"

I didn't finish the sentence before about thirty "volunteers" rushed forward. I had chaos and I hadn't even lifted the lid of the box! I pointed to a man with big muscles and said, "You, pass out the sandwiches while I hold back the line." Things were going comparatively well for a minute or so, when suddenly I heard a loud splash…my muscle-man helper had been thrown into the lake!

As quickly as he was thrown in, he jumped out. Within seconds, he had a hard wooden stick in his hands. Then, like a wet and fiery-eyed Errol Flynn in his prime, he tensed his muscles and went for the culprit who had tossed him into the lake.

The tosser looked terrified. Preferring chaos to murder, I picked up the box of food and ran. I thought that if I took away what they were there for, it would break up the fight. It worked. The crowd, including Errol Flynn, ran after me. I turned to him, put my hand on his wet shoulder and said, "This man, in the line of duty, *was thrown into the lake at MacArthur Park!*" (a fate almost worse than death). Then I thrust a double portion of food into his hands. He smiled and the crowd laughed.

It was around that time that we saw a man with a knife chasing someone (the incident I mentioned in Chapter 1). After that, I had second thoughts about taking females to the park with no men but myself. It certainly was a "place of death," so I eased off for a while until I felt that God wanted me to go back. That time came three months later. I took a team of a dozen Christians including two nurses.

When we arrived, I looked around for familiar faces and saw my old friend Pop. He ran toward me, stopped, cupped his hands toward his mouth and yelled a heartwarming, *"It's Ray!"* He then gave me a big hug. It was nice to feel wanted.

I met a few new residents that day. As I stood up and spoke, one man whose name was Victor began heckling me. His interjections lacked a little in intellectual content. The main thrust of his contention was that I was a racist and a hypocrite. As far as he was concerned, I was solely responsible for all the racial problems in the world, as well as the hypocrisy in the Church. Victor was a very angry man. My soft answer didn't turn away his wrath, nor did the fact that I loaded him up with food.

Gruesome Work

Having a team of helpers was a real boost for the ministry. Debbie, a member of the team, had been particularly helpful by calling hospitals to get donations of medicine and bandages. In fact, the response was so good that we had to have a truck move the supplies from our home to another location because they were taking up so much room.

Debbie and her husband, Jerry, decided to join our team even though Jerry had a habit of fainting at the sight of human blood. Debbie also had her own not-too-little inhibitions about ministering at the park. The first time they came, we had a mass of wounds to tend. She found herself dressing the crushed skull of a lady who had been hit on the head with a bottle. It was particularly gruesome because Beth noticed what looked like "gray matter" in the wound.

As the team ministered to the sick, I began to move around the park. I found Victor sitting on a seat, so I sat next to him. No matter how kind I tried to be, he had nothing but hatred toward me. This didn't please a restless resident who could hear what was going on. He had a heavy stick in his hand and without warning brought it down on the wooden bench next to us, sounding very much like a gun going off. That made things worse. Now Victor was angry and very nervous. He told me to tell my supporter to leave. I assured the gentleman that I could handle the situation myself.

I had to buy back food that I had originally given to Victor, in order to share with this hungry man.

Just then a lean-looking man came up to me and asked for food. He was really hungry and all the food was gone—that is, all the food except for the pile Victor had on his lap. This was Victor's opportunity to show me up for the hypocrite I was—he could shame me by sharing some of his food with a hungry member of his own race. I humbly asked him if he would be kind enough to share. *Share?* Was I kidding? Victor McScrooge would only give his brother food *if I paid him for it!*

That's just what happened. I had to buy back food that I

had originally given to Victor, in order to share with this hungry man. Victor had not a plank but a California Redwood in his eye.

During that time, I came to know one of the police officers in the park. While we were giving out food, two squad cars pulled up, and two officers grabbed a guy who was looking over the clothing we had brought. The police knew what they were doing. They immediately made him put his hands on his head, then reached under his jacket and relieved him of an eight-inch knife that was tucked into his belt. Somehow during the arrest, one of the policemen cut himself and had to have his hand bandaged, something one does not take lightly with AIDS so prevalent in a place like MacArthur Park.

The officer I spoke with was very compassionate toward those in the park. It is easy to say that these people need to "get themselves a job," but who in his right mind would hire a homeless person with a crack habit? Where does someone go who can't afford the high rents of Southern California? Their choice is to either wander the streets of Los Angeles or live in the park.

It Never Rains in California

It had been a freezing cold week. Snow had fallen throughout Northern California due to arctic weather that found its way down the country. People donated warm clothes and gave so generously that our garage was filled with them. When the freeze set in, I couldn't help thinking of those at the park. They were cold at night even in normal winter temperatures. Yet the day we were due to go, it poured—*man*, it poured.

It more than poured, it blew. I couldn't imagine anyone staying around the park in such conditions, so I canceled that day's trip. I told a team member named Mike that I would probably go on the following Monday.

On Monday the weather was fine. The rain had left the Los Angeles air clean and crisp. I waited awhile for a call from Mike, but with half the morning gone, I concluded that he couldn't make it. It appeared that it would be like old times, trying to give out food by myself. After loading up the car, I went to my office to print a document and make some photocopies, then went down to our church's food bank to get some food. The church had recently started a free food distribution program and they made an unlimited amount of food available to us for the park residents.

As I pulled into the parking lot, Mike rushed toward my car carrying his shoes and socks. He was in such a hurry to catch me that he didn't take time to put them on. He related that he called my home, found out that I'd left, and rushed down to the church to catch up with me. He had also called Beth, so this day I would have two helpers.

On the way to the park, we stopped and fed Tom. He was still at the same bus stop, and it had been over a year since I'd first seen him. As we walked toward him, he had his shoe off and was cleaning his foot with a black brush. The foot was red and scarred. I could understand why he wore a leg brace as his ankle was also horribly scarred. It turned out that he'd been hit by a bus some years earlier. We loaded him up with food, including a large box of candy, prayed for him and left. I felt frustrated that even though we had befriended Tom, he was still in the same state he had been in for years. What we needed was some sort of home into which we could place the "Toms" of L.A. This would help them to be in a position to get jobs and live with some dignity.

As we were unloading the car at the park, a tall man in his mid-twenties stopped us and asked, "Are you giving these people clothes?" When I replied that we were, he said, "That's really weird. I was just thinking about going home and getting some of my own clothes to give to these people!" He then asked if he could help. He put his cigarette out and picked up a box of clothes. At the call to repentance, he stepped forward to give his life to Christ. He turned out to be an actor from Pasadena. He was in good company; there were plenty of good actors standing in front of me.

Shortly after that, Beth and I were talking to a woman in her fifties who had very red, swollen hands. In fact, they were so inflamed from the crack she was on that she was in tears. Suddenly I heard hysterical cries from behind me. A girl in her teens was weeping so much, she was hyperventilating almost to the point of fainting. I left the older lady in Beth's capable hands.

I found out that this girl's boyfriend had gotten her pregnant, and he had other women beat her stomach with a baseball bat to try to kill the child. As I held her in my arms, I asked her, "Is he still your boyfriend?"

She sniffed and weakly replied, "No."

I asked, "Do you want me to get you out of this place?"

Again she whispered, "No!" then got up, and like an injured and frightened animal, she ran away.

As we were leaving that day, I saw someone lying on the ground, involved in the "battle of the blanket." He was trying to wrap a blanket around his body and it wouldn't quite fit. As I approached him, he finally seemed to get comfortable as he lay in the dirt. I asked, "Do you want me to 'tuck you in'?" He looked up at me and smiled from ear to ear.

I wondered if I would have smiled if our places were changed.

Wall Street

I was away ministering in another state on Saturday, but the team seemed to do okay without me. One member, Steve, admitted feeling a little apprehensive that one of the listeners cleaned his fingernails with a long blade as he preached. On the same day, a guy with a knife chased someone but was prevented from killing him by others at the park. Instead, he crept up on the guy he wanted to stab and hit him on the head with a wooden chair. The victim suffered a concussion so the team took him to a hospital.

Dave, another team member, said that he offered a girl a tract and she refused. He offered it to her twice more. Steve approached Dave a little later and advised him to ease off, because he overheard her say that if Dave offered her that tract one more time, she was going to kill him. The long machete blade she was holding under her coat gave credibility to her threat. I'm sure that if we knew how many knives were hidden under clothing, we would have wanted to visit some other place.

He overheard her say that if Dave offered her that tract one more time, she was going to kill him.

I once arrived with the team and made my way into a group of about a hundred very busy shoppers. In fact, that area looked like Wall Street on a heavy trading day. As I directed the team to bring over the food and clothing, a local approached me and whispered, "You know me . . . I'm your friend. A guy was murdered here two days ago. There are guns and knives here. *They're selling crack and they wouldn't like you to speak right here. I think they would shoot you.*" I moved our location about sixty feet to the side of Wall Street.

The previous week, Steve was due to speak but got lost on the way to the park. The team lined up about a hundred hungry people and waited for him. After quite some time,

Chuck felt he had better do something, so he preached to them while they were in line. It worked; nobody moved.

This day I waited until everyone was in line and had been given candy before I preached the gospel. At the challenge to come forward, four people stepped out of the line to give their lives to Christ. One of them was James, my muscular Errol Flynn–like helper, who had been thrown into the lake.

After the food was given out, I walked around the park. I saw a few regulars, including one man I barely recognized. He was fading away.

As we talked, "Snow" drifted by. I hadn't seen her for months. She was the one who told me to watch my back the first day I spoke in the crack area. She lifted both her hands and said, "Just visiting!"

I called, "Not buying?"

She shook her head, smiled and said, "No." Snow was pure.

As she walked off into the distance, a guy seated near me grunted, "She's selling."

Just then, a police car appeared in the distance and began to slowly meander through the park. I looked over to Wall Street and saw that not only had trading stopped, but the whole area was deserted.

It was a good day. Several people had made commitments to Christ. Victor Logeye had even smiled at me, and as I left, Pop called out, "I love you, Ray."

Waiting for the "rush."

The gang fight sequence. The man on the right has an axe in his hand; the rival gang member on the left has a knife.

He passes the axe to another gang member.

He then hits the rival with the axe. The man wasn't seriously injured.

The first time Ray preached open-air in the U.S. (Honolulu, Hawaii, 1985).

Somebody's daughter, high at MacArthur Park.

A quick, shaky picture of a drug deal (someone spotted the camera).

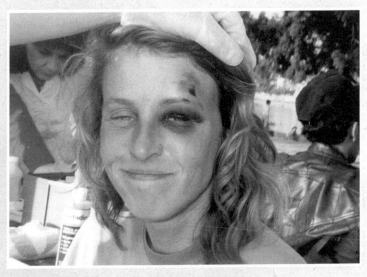

A head wound and a black eye received in a fight over 25 cents.

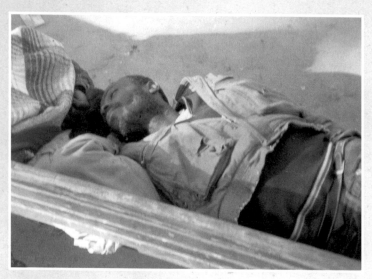

Sleeping off a high.

Crack cocaine being smoked openly at the park.

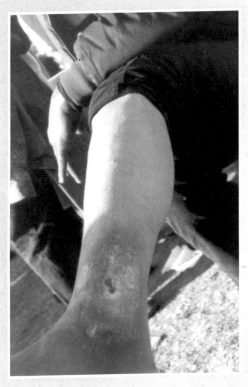

A typical
MacArthur Park
leg wound.

Dreaming of the next fix.

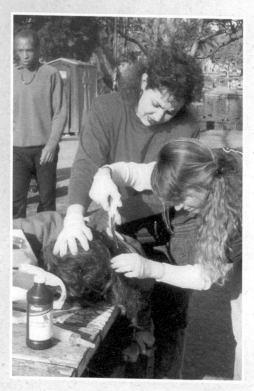

Cutting away hair to get to a head wound.

The head wound bandaged.

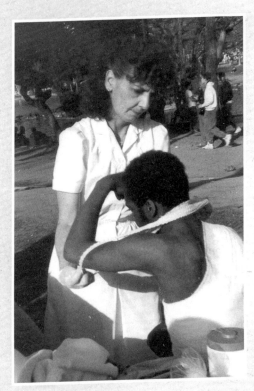

Stab wounds were common at MacArthur Park.

Preacher's-eye view at the Manti Pageant.
Miss Verbal is top left.

*Pop having a
bite to eat.*

Brenda at Stab Alley.

Tom, sitting in his usual position at the bus stop.

Tom, after some Christian love and a little Comfort.

The man with the 4-foot steel pipe "baseball bat" hit the rib cage of his opponent with the force of a home run.

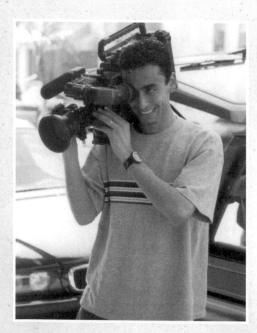

Emeal Zwayne (EZ) trying out the video camera.

A heckler in
Venica Beach, CA.

Mark Spence, Ray, and Kirk Cameron.

CHAPTER 14

STAB ALLEY

On one hand I felt happy; on the other hand I was saddened. The police busted MacArthur Park for thirty days. Day after day, masses of officers went to the park arresting anyone they deemed suspicious. Then they stayed there. *And then they placed a police substation in the park.* The effect was powerful. The "Armpit" had been scrubbed and deodorized. Suddenly my ministry was gone.

I called the Union Rescue Mission and asked Alex where the homeless gathered in L.A. His reply was immediate: "Go to 5th Street in downtown L.A. You will find about two thousand homeless on the streets in that area."

He was right. When I took a team there, hundreds lined up on the sidewalk seconds after we stopped the vehicle. If MacArthur Park was an armpit, this was the pit of the other arm of the homeless. It had that same familiar smell, but the smell was outweighed by the fact that I had an instant crowd. I began taking a team there each Saturday I was in town.

The Red Rag

The gang problem in L.A. was out of control. At that time there were over 750 gangs in the county, with 750,000 members, the average age being sixteen years. They were recruiting kids as young as eight or nine. Every weekend, without fail, there were multiple gang killings. It was not unusual to have seven or eight gang members killed in one weekend, along with a mother shot or a child killed in a drive-by shooting. There were even tragic stories of people being shot and killed *just because they were wearing the wrong color clothing.* Gangs are known by their different colors. If an innocent party finds himself wearing a blue shirt in a red area, that can be his death. One poor man found himself lost one day while driving, and ended up on a street that was literally a dead end: he was shot to death. The same thing happened to an innocent family in the mid '90s.

When Ken, a lieutenant-sheriff who attended our church, asked if I would be interested in visiting the Los Angeles County Jail, I jumped at the opportunity.

Since the jail was in the downtown area, I decided to stop at 5th Street on the way. Ken had previously asked if he could join our outreach, so it was a chance to kill two birds with one stone. Two other friends decided they would also like to tour the jail.

Within two minutes of parking on 5th Street, a crowd of about one hundred, mainly men, lined up for food. The previous time I spoke they seemed very restless, so I decided to try some sleight-of-hand. The most effective in my repertoire at that time was the "disappearing rag" trick.

I took my red rag in my right hand, put it into my left hand and made it disappear. Were they impressed! Then I made it appear again before speaking on the fact that the eyes aren't trustworthy.

For the first time in weeks, I had their undivided attention. I could hear people saying, "How'd you do dat?"—"Do dat again..." So I did. I took the red rag from my right hand and put it into my left. Then I spoke, we gave out food, and got back into the van.

As Ken sat in the passenger seat, he looked at me with a rather sober expression and said, "Next time you do that trick, use a *green* rag." It suddenly dawned on me what I had just done. While I was doing the trick, he could hear voices saying, "This is a blue neighborhood!" and "That's a *red* rag!" I hadn't merely worn a red shirt, but I had waved a red rag in their faces like a mad bullfighter standing in front of a herd of angry bulls!

Ken had a different attitude than most as we gave out the food. He didn't mind that many were so deceitful that they would sneak around the back of the line for more, or that they would take food for themselves and let others go hungry. After twenty years in law enforcement, he knew that each of those men who took food would stab you in the back as quickly as look at you. Although I didn't like to think much about it, I knew he was right.

Twenty-three thousand people were housed in the jail system at that time; six thousand were in the building in which Ken worked. After surrendering our driver's licenses for ID, we began our tour. It was a sobering sight to see so many human beings indebted to the law.

Nowadays, as new customers are welcomed into the jail, authorities have a complete history of where they are from and their criminal record. If they place a "Crip" in a cell full of "Bloods," that's what they will have on their hands. But now, thanks to the press of a computer key, a Crip can be housed with other Crips.

There were also separate cells for suicidal inmates, crazy

inmates, murderers, and those going through drug withdrawal. We walked in front of men who were trophies of hell— men who mumbled nonsensical words at us as we walked by their cages. One grabbed the bars of his eight-by-five-foot cell and screamed in torment that he needed help for his mental condition. I felt overwhelmed with pity. Then he angrily went into a spiel about how he hated blacks, before quickly shifting gears and saluting the officers who were showing us around.

As they pushed, I felt a hand in my back pocket. Someone had a hand on my wallet!

We looked into the death row cells as well as a series of windowless rooms in which special prisoners were kept. As we came out, one of the officers commented that very few people were allowed in there. When I asked why we were allowed in, he replied, "Well, you're not going to give them anything!" I don't think he noticed the prisoner reading a tract that I had slipped to him.

It was only after an hour or so of hearing everyone call Ken "Sir" that I learned he was the boss of his area. His job was to prepare the thousand new customers brought in to the prison system each day.

I felt as though I were looking back into the seventeenth century as I peered at approximately a hundred and fifty men who were chained to each other. They were then unchained and herded into a room where they were categorized and strip-searched.

More than once as I passed groups of prisoners, I would say, "Hiya, guys," and get a warm response from some. Others would stare back with the warmth of dry ice.

Persistent Pocket Picker

Back on 5th Street, I finished speaking about the subject of abortion and heard one man grit his teeth in moral outrage and say, "If one of my women had an abortion, I'd kill her!"

That day we had a number of jackets and sleeping bags to give to the homeless, and it caused a near riot. The previous week, bargain hunters knocked me to the ground. I was a little short on helpers so I asked that twelve men stand in a semi-circle while I put boxes of clothing on the sidewalk. The men kept back the crowd, but as each saw something he fancied, he moved slightly forward.

I could see the feet of the men inching their way closer until suddenly, instead of being protected by a wall of men, I was under their shadow. Then I was on the ground, as they, and the crowd they should have been holding back, dove at the pile of clothing.

This day, there were so many people around the back of the van that I couldn't get the door open after I had finished speaking. I told Rachel and her friend, Beckie, to get into the vehicle as the situation seemed to be heating up. They opened a window and began frantically passing clothing to me from inside the van.

Suddenly I had twenty to thirty people pushing from behind me and grabbing the clothes even before I got them out of the window. As they pushed, *I felt a hand in my back pocket.* Someone had a hand on my wallet! I'd forgotten to leave it hidden in the van. I grabbed the hand, but whoever it was wouldn't let go. I turned around and yelled, "Let go of my wallet!" and felt the hand pulling back. There were so many pushing and shoving that I couldn't figure out who it belonged to.

After giving out food so many times, we finally found a system that worked. Food went into opaque plastic bags so that no one knew what they, or the person in front of them, received. This stopped hungry people from rioting when they saw their favorite food. The bags were tied at the top so that no one could see inside, keeping complaints to a minimum if they happened to be disappointed. When they lined up, they were told to stay where they were, while we moved the van twenty feet down the street. After speaking to them, we piled the food on the sidewalk and then released people individually from the single line after handing each a tract. One person had the job of maintaining the single-file line; two people gave out tracts and released individuals for food. Another person kept the twenty-foot area clear, and two handed out the food. We then began dropping the clothing out of the back of the van while it was moving.

The following week, I saw a woman who was a dwarf walking down the sidewalk minutes before I was due to speak. She was a sorry sight. Her tiny bare feet were blackened with dirt. I put my arm around her and tried to get her to stay and listen, but she wasn't hungry and said she would come back. When we left that day, I saw her sitting on the sidewalk in an area we called "Stab Alley." It was the pit of pits.

When we drove through Stab Alley the next Saturday, she was sitting in the same area. I stopped the van and went over to her with a blanket. She was out of it. I shook her for about twenty seconds until finally she opened one eye. Then I gave her the blanket and told her to hide it so it wouldn't be stolen while she slept. When I returned to the van, Debbie had taken her sneakers off and asked if she could give them to her. I thought they would be too big because the woman's feet were only about five inches long, but I decided to take them over anyway. Another member of the team took $10 out of his wallet and offered it, but I said she would just use it for cocaine.

As I approached her, she was lying with one eye half open. Suddenly she saw the sneakers, lunged forward and grabbed them, at the same time crossing herself at least four times and saying, "Thank you, Jesus!" over and over. It was so moving I almost cried. The only thing I could compare it to would be a man dying of thirst, reacting to water being handed to him. As she held the sneakers, I slipped my socks off and put them on her little feet, followed by the sneakers. Then I went back to the car and got the $10 from Tom, along with a Gospel of John, folded the bill up and tucked it into her tiny hand. She was so pleased, she didn't know how to express herself.

The next time I spoke, I told of a man in England who was arrested for being a kingpin in the drug world. Police found an expensive calculator in his possession, and as they took it from him he bragged, "You won't find any drug transactions on that, because I've erased them completely."

The law however took the calculator back to the manufacturer and, because it was an expensive model, it contained a very sophisticated memory bank.

The makers were then able to summon every single transaction. The man got twenty years in prison.

My point was to warn them that we may have forgotten the sins of our youth, but each of us has a very sophisticated memory bank within our calculating minds called the "subconscious." It has recorded every sin against God's Law as well as every sight that has passed before our eyes, every sound that has entered our ears, and every thought within our mind. Proof of this is the experience of having a song from our youth immediately recall memories of things we did that we thought we had totally forgotten.

At the thought of standing before God on Judgment Day, we have the delusion that we have nothing to fear because we've removed every transgression from the mind. We think the Law has nothing on us. We don't realize that we will be going back to the Manufacturer who will bring everything out into the open as evidence of our guilt, "including every secret thing, whether it is good or whether it is evil" (Ecclesiastes 12:14).

Of course, not everyone paid attention. There was a lot of noise. Some listened, some talked, and the rest didn't speak English. But there were always people who wanted Gospels of John and tracts when I finished speaking.

Another time when I had been there with a friend, I stood on the road to preach to those lying and sitting on the sidewalk. Someone started a lawnmower just as I began, and turned it off when I finished.

As we walked along the road back to the van that day, a police car cruised by and an officer asked sarcastically, "Something wrong with the sidewalk?" I stopped myself from saying that there was: it had a strong stench of urine, with dirty bodies, blankets, cardboard, and stinking trash strewn over it.

A few weeks later as we were driving down Stab Alley, Debbie saw Brenda, the little lady we had spoken to earlier. We walked the full length of Stab Alley to get to her. People were openly smoking crack as we walked past them. I felt for Debbie as we made our way down the alley; lots of eyes were gazing at the two of us. I gave a friendly, "How ya doin'?" to different people as we walked by, which seemed to ease the tension. Just as we saw Brenda, I was distracted by a girl who called out, "I know you—you're from MacArthur Park!" It was one of the park's regulars, although I barely recognized her. Her arms were so skinny and her face so gaunt.

Brenda was pleased to see us. She had gone to the hospital, she told us, and while she was there someone had stolen her bag containing her Bible and the sneakers Debbie gave her. She may have been telling the truth...then again, she may have sold them for crack or alcohol. God knows.

We gave her another Gospel of John and some women's personal things, then prayed with her. Debbie closed her eyes when we prayed; I didn't. I was watching out for both of our backs. Hundreds of drug users were right behind us.

Demons were also present. One man qualified as the most raving demon-possessed man I had ever seen. A 5th Street regular, he was constantly talking to himself (or themselves) in an angry tone. Whenever I spoke to him, it was always with a soft answer.

That same day he angrily said he was allergic to the food we gave him. Then he began talking to his reflection in our van's window, saying he was going to smash its windows.

He stood directly behind us while Debbie prayed.

All this didn't faze Debbie, though. The next day she looked after the nursery at our church, and said that it was *worse* than Stab Alley.

Streetwise

One Saturday, a friend named Jeff came with us to 5th Street. He was very streetwise and was able to fill me in on the use of cocaine. Now in his mid-twenties, Jeff had started using drugs when he was eleven years old. His mother was a dealer before she tragically died. He moved from pills, to powder cocaine, then on to crack cocaine, and into crime (including robbery). After he was converted in 1989, he had a real compassion for those on the street.

On the way down to 5th Street, he enlightened me about the difference between crack and coke. The conventional powder cocaine can give a thirty- to forty-minute high, while crack, which is far more addictive, gives only a thirty- to sixty-*second* "buzz." That's why it works out to be so expensive—$50 goes nowhere. I asked him what the buzz was like and his answer was not surprising. "I really don't know how to put this, Ray, but there's no other way of describing it: it's like [sex]."

What young man could resist such temptation? If cocaine became flesh, I'm sure she would be a beautiful whore, reminiscent of the harlot young men are warned about in the wisdom of Solomon: "I perceived among the youths, a young man devoid of understanding...And there a woman met him...So she caught him and kissed him...she said, 'Let us delight ourselves with love.'...With her flattering lips she seduced him...He did not know it would take his life... Pay attention to the words of my mouth: Do not let your heart turn aside to her ways, do not stray into her paths; for she has cast down many wounded, and all who were slain by her were strong men. Her house is the way to hell, descending to the chambers of death" (Proverbs 7:7–27).

As usual when we arrived, a line formed before we even got out of the van. As I was getting out, a thin man in a gangster-style hat picked a four-foot steel bar out of the trash can, and casually stood at the front of the line. I didn't take much notice. I walked across and stood where I usually speak.

Suddenly there was shouting about someone jumping the line, and the man pulled the steel bar back and swung it full force like a baseball bat into another man's rib cage. I waved at Jeff to ignore his instincts and keep back from the fight, then checked that the women on the team were okay. The man who was hit had to be restrained for about two minutes. He then disappeared, and—surprise!—back he came with a garden hoe in his hands.

After a few threats and shouts from the crowd to *"Cool it, man!"* he backed down, then it was all over.

After I spoke, we drove around to Stab Alley and gave

Brenda some food. When I asked if she had a crack habit, her look said, "How could you even *think* such a thing?" She did, however, admit to a wine habit. When I asked if she would like me to find someone at our church to take her in, she seemed quite happy to stay where she was.

On the way back home Jeff said he thought Brenda was telling the truth. Apparently her face wasn't thin enough for her to be on crack, and besides, she would have been down on the other end of the street where crack was sold.

Lonny, one of the other team members, said he thought the blow with the steel bar would have knocked the man to the ground. Jeff filled us in again. If the man had fallen, he would have received another five blows, at least, while he was down. I had seen that sort of thing. When a man is hit and falls to the ground, it becomes a "dog eat underdog" situation. I saw one man holding another on the ground by sitting on his chest while he mercilessly punched him in the face four or five times.

The reason the man came back with the garden hoe was to let the aggressor know that he wasn't going to just take it, and decline in the pecking order. That's being streetwise.

I respected Jeff's opinion—adding to his credibility were the scars from a stab wound on his chest and a bullet wound on his arm.

Frown, You're on Candid Camera

One day, Jesse, a member of the team, wanted to take a video camera to 5th Street to show his wife what it was like. I said it would be fine, but told him not to get out of the van until I told the crowd what he was up to.

Only three people in a line of about one hundred and fifty objected to being filmed, so I said they could either leave or hide their faces when the camera pointed toward them.

Things went fine until Jesse asked if he could film Stab Alley. I said I thought it would be fine; no one had objected so far, so no one would object if we went around the corner, right? Wrong. *Very* wrong!

As soon as we rounded the corner, all hell broke loose. It was as though we had shined a bright flashlight into a rat-infested room. People began running, some away from us, some toward us. Someone yelled, "Hey, a camera... *get that outta here!*" A number of people pulled their sweaters over their faces; others held their hands up. I could see a lot of anger and fear in a lot of eyes.

I heard someone else yell, "Whites!" The atmosphere was not a good one. It felt like a few people were about to be murdered. We left, *pronto!*

All hell broke loose. It was as though we had shined a bright flashlight into a rat-infested room.

Minutes later, we returned camera-less. Little Brenda seemed a different person as we knelt in front of her. Her voice was gruff as she spoke. Happy had turned into Grumpy. She held onto an unlit cigarette as she rummaged through a cardboard box of belongings. The sidewalk on which she sat was filthy. On her lap was a small steel blade in case anyone hassled her. Once again Jeff filled me in on why she was in such a bad disposition. Some get their government check each month, spend it all, and have a few days of bliss. They are popular and find themselves surrounded by friends. Then, when the cash and drugs run out, they are left with a hollow despair. Brenda wasn't the only one in a bad mood that day.

In an effort to take away the feeling of despair, they beg or buy cheap wine to drown their sorrows. Then comes the craving for alcohol. This was Jeff's experience. He said people caught in this vicious cycle don't know what they're doing to themselves until they look in the mirror after six months. He used to smoke crack all night, then start drinking wine at 6 a.m.

He spoke of a time when he and his friends sold some "48 fake" (dummy cocaine), made with "cooked up" old candle wax and baking soda. They bought a substance from the drugstore that numbs the tongue, and put it on the fake rock. The prospective buyer tastes it, considers it genuine cocaine, and buys it. The seller walks off laughing; he now has cash to purchase real crack, to get high and happy, while the customer just gets low and angry. Jeff once sold a batch of 48 fake for over $100, but his customers came back and found him. They were in a truck, and were so outraged that they drove up on the sidewalk and ran over a girl Jeff was standing with, breaking her legs, arm, and rib.

One of Jeff's friends had a steady, well-paying job in Long Beach. In the evenings he would buy crack and smoke it. Someone who didn't like him sold him some bad crack. He died in the middle of the street.

Little did I know that my little friend, Brenda, would be killed by a truck a year later as she walked down Stab Alley.

CHAPTER 15

A REBELLIOUS CHILD

It continually amazes me how God can bring an individual out of a life of darkness and into His marvelous light. The life of one young man, who is now dear to me, is one such example.

It was the early 1990s. A fifteen-year-old named Emeal Zwayne was in the midst of cutting a rap demo with a Hollywood recording studio, and had signed a contract with successful producers. That wasn't the only contract he had put his name to. Emeal had just joined the infamous street gang known as the Crips.

Sometime earlier, he had walked off his school campus in Southern California, went to an alley not far from the school, and been viciously beaten by four gang members as part of the initiation ceremony.

Emeal, known to his friends as EZ, had been elected class

president during his freshman year of high school. He wanted popularity, and he had it. He was a tough kid who did not hesitate to threaten to kill one of his teachers. He had also been caught vandalizing a classroom, and by the middle of his sophomore year, he had already been kicked out of two high schools.

EZ was born in Lebanon. In the late 1970s, he watched as his mother, distraught at the thought of EZ's teenage brother going to war, locked the front door of the house and hid the key. As his determined brother headed toward the door, his mother grabbed hold of the Army shirt that he held in his hand. Undeterred, he continued toward the door, dragging her across the floor, then he kicked open the locked door and fled into the darkness of war.

Other than that dramatic incident, EZ didn't remember much about his war-torn country. Most of his memories were rooted in the United States. Shortly after the incident with his brother, his family immigrated to the U.S. They came to the conclusion that Lebanon didn't hold much of a future for the family.

EZ's young life was steeped in Roman Catholicism. He kept many of the church's rituals and often partook of Holy Communion. But there was a rebellious spirit in this child, who had been influenced by a brother with a soldier's mentality. He had been taught to be tough, and had developed a strong animosity toward anyone different from himself.

This animosity manifested itself even in kindergarten, where he would grab other children in chokeholds and became known as a thief and a troublemaker.

His rebellion wasn't confined to the classroom. When an aunt and uncle came to visit, they were very concerned that their van was in danger of being vandalized. They were right. It was in danger, but not from strangers. After hearing of their concern, EZ went outside and jumped on it, broke off the windshield wipers, scratched it, then snapped off the antenna. Then he went inside and said with wide eyes, "Someone has vandalized your van!" He did this more than once.

When he went to elementary school, he found that he could impress friends by lying to them about being a monarch from another country. He told them that he had come into the United States for refuge. As he grew, he continued to fight, lie, steal, and vandalize cars.

Collecting for the Scouts

One day he put on a Cub Scout uniform and went around his neighborhood collecting money for handicapped kids. He pocketed the money.

The strange irony was that EZ didn't want to be a bad kid. As an eight-year-old, he had decided to clean up his life. He wanted to be a good Catholic, so he had tried to stop lying, stealing, and cussing. He even prayed at night, wore a cross, and began reading a children's Bible.

But it wasn't long until the dark part of his heart began to dominate his young life. He drifted from the church and back into his lies. He acquired a consistent track record of suspensions from elementary school and junior high for "inappropriate behavior."

When he entered high school, things really became bad. It was as though he had no conscience. He began drinking, experimenting with marijuana, and doing other things that come with the lifestyle. He started ditching classes and lying to teachers. Near the end of his sophomore year he had four F's and two D minuses. He didn't even deserve the D's; two teachers had been overly gracious. His grade point average was a mere 0.32. He was finally expelled when he was caught writing graffiti on the school walls.

A Stirred Conscience

It was getting close to Mother's Day. EZ's family had gathered at his parents' home. One of his sisters from New Jersey had traveled across the country to surprise the family with the news that she was pregnant.

As they talked, another sister took the time to tell her younger brother that he needed to clean up his life. She told EZ that he was worthless. Something in the young man snapped. He jumped up, grabbed a knife from a kitchen drawer, and began stabbing himself in the wrist. Fortunately, the knife was dull and didn't do any major damage. He did, however, upset his visiting sister. She was so distraught by the incident that she miscarried the child.

The baby's death left an indelible impression on EZ. He became even worse and found himself thinking of suicide. His conscience was bothering him. He knew that he wasn't right with God and was terrified that his lifestyle was taking him to hell.

A Stunned Mom

Bill was EZ's best friend. His life had taken him in a different direction than that of the young gangster. Late one evening, both Bill and EZ got drunk. In the early hours of the morning, EZ turned to Bill and said, "This is the best feeling I've ever had. I want to feel this way the rest of my life!"

Bill's parents had invited both boys to a crusade. Later that day, EZ told his mom, "I'm going to a Christian thing with Bill." Her reaction was to snap back, "You liar! I know what you are up to!" For one of the few times in his life, EZ was telling the truth. Her reaction angered him, and he let her know it by punching the wall.

He was still fuming on the way to the meeting. When he entered the auditorium, the sight of 23,000 people and the sound of the music began to soften his heart. That night this rebellious young man realized that he was a sinner. For the first time in his life he heard that eternal life was a gift. In response to the altar call, he jumped up and ran forward, tears streaming down his face. He could hardly believe that God could forgive him for all the things he had done. In a moment of time, he was transformed.

A New Life

EZ became a new creation, and the transformation was immediately apparent. As he got into the car to leave the crusade, the radio came on. He immediately turned it off. He now didn't want to listen to music that glorified sex and violence.

When he arrived home, he remembered the fight he had had with his mother. As he gazed through the window, he could see by her expression that she was still fuming. He didn't realize that it wasn't just the fight that had upset her. His mother had found out that night that he had been stealing, and she was about to throw him out of the house.

EZ said a cheery "Hi, Mom" as he walked through the doorway. Her face looked grim. When she confronted him about his stealing, she was stunned that he immediately confessed to his crimes.

As they began talking, EZ told her about everything he had been involved in. He also found out later that there had been times when she had locked her bedroom door because she was afraid that he would kill her. He looked deeply into her eyes and said, "Mom, mark these words: *nothing will ever be the same again.*"

Nothing was the same. He knocked on some of the doors of the neighbors down his street and apologized to them for his former lifestyle. He also called his record producer and told him that as a Christian, he could no longer rap. He knew that he couldn't be two people—one on-stage and another off-stage. He was duly released from the contract.

Then he contacted his gang and informed them that he had to get out, even if it meant being beaten up. They told him, "We don't want anything to do with this God stuff. You are out. We're not going to jump you."

EZ had another problem. Before the crusade, he had organized a cocaine deal. He was also at the point of placing an order for a gun. When he didn't show up to make the trade, he later learned that one of the two dealers had decided to kill him.

EZ called them to explain that he had become a Christian. Their reaction stunned him: "So are we. We go to Bible study and to church, but we still have to make a living." They too let him off the hook.

He then went back to the first school that had expelled him and pleaded with them to take him back. It seemed that it wouldn't be an easy thing to do. The principal had once said to his brother, "If EZ ever comes back to this school, I will quit my job."

Fortunately, the principal was impressed enough with EZ's sincerity to have an administrative meeting to consider his request. Then he called and said, "We will send you to a continuation school. If you do okay for the first semester, we will take you back for the second."

He did "okay." In fact, he was voted the most improved male student on campus. At a special banquet to which his mom and dad were invited, he was given an award. One of the principals was taken aback with the change. She asked, "What got into you?" EZ beamed as he answered, "The Lord." She smiled and welcomed him back.

One of the school supervisors wasn't so convinced. When she was told that EZ was returning to school, she said, "No way! I can't stand him."

Her fears soon proved unfounded. EZ quickly became a Bible study leader, and his grade point average went from 0.32 to 4.0—straight A's.

After finishing high school, he attended a Bible university, majoring in biblical studies and theology. He then became an ordained pastor at the age of twenty. Truly, the Lord had changed him and nothing was ever the same again!

What's in a Name?

In June 1995, EZ was the guest speaker at a church retreat, when a woman told him there was something on her heart that she needed to share with him. That seemed a little strange in itself, because she didn't know him very well. But she also said that she couldn't yet tell him what she was supposed to.

A short time later one Saturday afternoon, EZ was reading his Bible. As he neared the end of Genesis chapter 24, his eyes fell upon the final verse: "Then Isaac brought her into his mother Sarah's tent; and he took Rebekah and she became his wife, and he loved her. So Isaac was comforted after his mother's death" (verse 67).

EZ identified with the verse, because his beloved mother had passed away eighteen months earlier. He had read this passage several times, yet this time was unlike any other, especially as he had mistakenly read the name Rebekah as Rachel. This would prove to be significant a short time later. He meditated on the verse for a moment, closed his Bible and said, "Lord, I pray that you will bring me a woman who will comfort me after the death of my mother."

Narrowing Down the Field

Around the time EZ's mother died, Rachel, my daughter, had looked at me and said, "Dad, when I get married, I want to marry someone who has a concern for the lost. I want him to be someone who preaches open-air and gives out gospel tracts." I smiled and thought, *Man! You have just narrowed down the field.* We had prayed that Rachel's husband would be a godly man. However, I didn't know too many eligible Christian young men who preached open-air. God, however, knew of one.

It was Sunday morning, the day after EZ had cried out to God for a wife. I had been invited to speak at a church in Yorba Linda, California. There were two services, and Rachel arrived before the second service to keep me company.

I didn't know too many eligible young men who preached open-air. God, however, knew of one.

I introduced her to a young man I had met named EZ. Then I deliberately went for a walk so they could get acquainted without her father being around.

A short time later, EZ received a call from the woman who had said she had something important to tell him. He remembered the conversation and was very interested in what she had to say. She told him, "It was on my heart to share with you from the passage in Genesis chapter 24, when Isaac met Rebekah, that God is going to bring you a woman who will comfort you after the death of your mother."

He was both shocked and overjoyed. He knew this woman had no idea that he had prayed about this very passage. However, he was confused because she had said "Isaac and Rebekah." EZ knew his Bible so he said, "Don't you mean Isaac and Rachel?"

She was adamant that she was right, so EZ suggested that he get his Bible and read the passage to her. As he did so, he almost had to wipe his eyes. The woman was right. When he read the passage, he had mistakenly read it as "Rachel."

Soon after this, Rachel began attending the church where EZ was now an assistant pastor. At one of the midweek services he happened to hear her say something that dumbfounded him. She said, "A lot of people mix up my name. Rather than calling me Rachel, they call me Rebekah." His mind suddenly raced back to how he had mixed up the two names. He knew that this was much more than a coincidence. From that point on he began to pray about Rachel becoming his wife.

For five long months, EZ kept the matter between himself and God. In the meantime, he developed a friendship with Rachel. One night, she walked into my prayer room after spending some time with him, and said, "Oh, Dad... I love him *so* much." EZ also loved Rachel, but during those months they never discussed their mutual affection.

Five months to the day after EZ asked God to bring him a woman to comfort him after the death of his mother, he revealed his love for Rachel. Three weeks later, they were engaged to be married.

Rachel's full name has great significance to the story. Her first name is Rachel, her middle name is Naomi, and her last name was Comfort. EZ had two previous serious relationships. One of the girls was named Rachel; the other was Naomi. Neither relationship gave him true comfort. However, God gave him another chance with Rachel Naomi, but this time with comfort. The day before he met his wife, he prayed that God would give him a woman of comfort. The following day God, in His great faithfulness, gave him Rachel Naomi Comfort.

Every father wants his daughter to be treated with respect. I found out after their honeymoon that EZ had driven out to the house where they were to stay in Palm Springs and filled a bowl with water and topped it with flower petals. When they arrived on their honeymoon, the first thing he did was wash my daughter's feet as a token of love and servitude.

Rachel received an answer to her prayer. EZ is one of the most zealous Christians I know. He not only gives out tracts like there is no tomorrow, but to date, he has visited over eight hundred homes in his area to reach his neighbors with the gospel. He has also preached open-air with me more than one hundred times.

Comfort and Love

It seems that God in His great faithfulness not only chose the right man for our daughter, but He also chose the right ladies for our two sons, Jacob and Daniel. When we first came to the United States, Jacob became friends with a young lady whose last name was "Love." He eventually married her. It was a Comfort-Love wedding. Then Daniel married her sister. Two Comforts married two Loves. It was very biblical: Jacob married Sarah and Daniel married Rebekah.

One of my favorite phrases to use in prayer is "I rest in Your faithfulness." The Bible tells us that "He who promised is faithful." In 2 Timothy 2:13 we are even told, "If we are faithless, He remains faithful; He cannot deny Himself." This is what I rested in when I prayed for the salvation of my unsaved parents and siblings. For over thirty years, I daily rested in the fact that I could rely on His faithfulness when it came to the eternal salvation of those I loved most.

My mom is Jewish. My dad, a Gentile, was open to the things of God and had even made a profession of faith (he would always come with me when I went anywhere to preach or to do atheist debates), but there was no fruit. Neither was he in fellowship or reading the Word of God. Like most people, however, he did pray.

On July 7, 2002, at 3:00 a.m., I received a long-distance call from New Zealand notifying me that my eighty-one-year-old dad had had a heart attack, fallen, and broken his hip. I cried bucket loads after the call. After he fell, he told my sister to tell me to pray for him. I called the hospital and after getting bad connections and being accidentally cut off, I got through on the sixth call and spoke to him. His heart was working at only 15 percent of its capacity. He was very weak and could hardly speak. When I told him that we were praying for him, he said, "I'm praying for you too."

I then said, "Dad, keep your faith in Jesus, won't you?"

He answered, "I'm going to."

My mom said she could see that he had a special peace, so she asked him if he had been born again. He replied that he had for some time, but didn't tell her because he didn't want to upset her. When a friend visited him, they prayed together. I called and asked my dad if he was happy about that. He whispered, "Very happy." He then said, "I want to pass on. I know I will be all right. I love you all." He died two weeks later.

At this point, my mom and siblings still are not saved. I'm not concerned, though. I rest in His faithfulness.

CHAPTER 16

A BIRD *in* *the* HAND

O n a visit to Hawaii, I spoke to a crowd of about a hundred and fifty people on the streets of Waikiki. During the preaching, a woman called out, "How can I be born again?" I thought to myself, *Another well-meaning Christian, trying to help by asking relevant questions —it is so obvious. What are you going to say next, "The wind blows where it wishes"?*

I was wrong. Her question was genuine, and she was led to the Savior that night.

As I walked back to the car with my friend Garry Ansdell, for some strange reason I said, "Let's stop and look at this tree." While we looked at the tree, he saw a white dove sitting on a branch about six feet off the ground. I stepped forward and, to my surprise, this gentle white bird let me take it in my hand. I concluded that it was injured, so I took

183

it with me, fed it, then it spent the night perched at the foot of my bed.

The next day it sat on the pulpit for an hour while I preached, and flew away that evening.

In Scripture the Holy Spirit is depicted as a dove. He is the Comforter—the One who stays with us in our darkest hours. It is my prayer that God will pour out His Spirit on the pulpits of this nation as He never has before, until our work on earth is done.

A great preacher once told the story of a governor who visited a prison and interviewed hundreds of criminals. They all claimed to be innocent and maintained that it wasn't their fault they were in prison—they were victims of society. It was their upbringing. Their plight was the fault of everyone else but themselves.

Then, to his surprise, he found one man who admitted he was in prison because he had broken the law. He said he deserved everything he had coming to him, and what he did was very wrong. The governor immediately left the prison, went back to his office, and sent a pardon to the prison authorities saying, "Get that man out of there immediately, *before he corrupts all those innocent men!*"

May God give to you honest sinners, who will admit their guilt in the midst of this crooked, perverse, and self-righteous generation. May He give you individuals who admit that they are Law-breakers so they will cry out, "How can I be born again?"

Feeding Crocodiles

One afternoon, Rachel caught an eight-inch lizard in our kitchen. "Will it bite me?" she wanted to know. I told her it wouldn't and got some honey to feed the creature.

I fed lizards with honey when I was a kid. They seemed

to appreciate free food. However, the lizards I fed as a child were a fraction of the size of this one.

As I put the wooden honey-laden stick near its mouth, it lunged out and grabbed it with its jagged teeth. Suddenly it looked like a vicious crocodile! I screamed, "Drop it—it'll bite you!" She did, and it scurried underneath the stove. We finally got the beast outside and let it go. It reminded me of an average day in downtown Los Angeles.

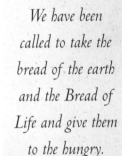

Feeding the homeless, preaching to the lost, and giving out literature and Bibles are often thankless tasks. Sometimes it may seem like feeding crocodiles. But that's what we have been called to do: to take the bread of the earth in one hand and the Bread of Life in the other and give them to the hungry.

We have been called to take the bread of the earth and the Bread of Life and give them to the hungry.

There are times when I would rather stay at home. I remember once attending a prayer meeting just before I was going out to 5th Street. Several members of the usual team called to say (for legitimate reasons) that they couldn't make it. So it looked as though there would be only two or three that day. I consoled myself with the thought that at least there were quite a number at the prayer meeting who could pray with me.

During the meeting, one by one people began to leave. Some had other things to do, but most left to attend a men's breakfast—quite legitimate also. However, there were soon only four left in the room. Then there were three—a friend named Robert, one lady, and me. I thought, *It's times like this that I cling to the promise, "Where two or three are gathered together in My name, I am there in the midst of them.*" Three people in prayer can be a powerhouse with God. I looked across at the woman who had her eyes closed, no doubt deep in prayer. Then I noticed her head was slightly to one side and her breathing was fairly loud—*she was asleep!*

Robert and I ended the prayer meeting in laughter. As I crept out, not wanting to disturb the men's breakfast, I couldn't help thinking, *Here are masses of men who come together for a breakfast, and I can't get even a handful to feed the homeless.* It was then that I determined to go by myself if necessary. When I arrived home, another call had come from someone who couldn't make it that day.

Jesus said that the laborers were few. The Bible asks the rhetorical question, "Who can find a faithful man?" Faithful men and women are few and far between. If we understand that, it will help keep us from becoming discouraged and cynical. There are probably so few laborers because we haven't been earnestly praying for them as Jesus told us to: "The harvest truly is great, but the laborers are few; therefore pray the Lord of the harvest to send out laborers into His harvest" (Luke 10:2).

A Christian friend once called me and earnestly said he needed to see me for counsel. When he came to my home, there was a sense of urgency in his voice. His "problem" was that he kept seeing everyone with the word "Death" written across their foreheads.

I said, "Hey, that's good!"

He replied, "No, it's not—it's bad, because I'm not witnessing to them. Pray for me!"

May that be the experience of you and me. May we see the people we don't know as potential friends in a holding cell with death waiting for them. May our conscience give us no rest until we take to them the pardon from heaven, and give them the key to unlock death's cold, black door.

God encouraged me on the day that I couldn't find laborers. Unexpectedly, three young men showed up at the last minute. Never forget that the Lord knows your struggles and that "God is not unjust to forget your work and labor of love" (Hebrews 6:10). He will encourage you when you need it.

Into the Lifeboat

After speaking at Ohio State University, I overheard a young woman say, "I'm a Christian. I believe that Jesus is Lord, but I don't think God will condemn everyone to hell. I think He is just." I asked her, "Do you share your faith?" She said, "No, I'm not a fundamentalist." Her erroneous belief was the cause of her inaction.

She was like a passenger in one of the *Titanic's* lifeboats. There is plenty of room in the lifeboat for others, but she deceives herself by dismissing any concern for those in the freezing water by thinking, *I don't believe they will drown. I really think they will survive the icy waters.* Those who think God is too kind to punish sin show their ignorance of Holy Scripture.

Earlier that day, I had been on a flight from Los Angeles to Chicago, seated next to a Roman Catholic couple. They asked what I did for a living, so I replied that I was an author and gave them each a book. They were very grateful. Then the woman asked, "What's the difference between a *born-again* Christian and a Christian?"

I told her that the phrase "born-again Christian" was redundant. It was like saying, "I'm a weatherman meteorologist." Both terms mean the same thing.

She asked, "How did you get born again?" Then she quizzed me about who led me to the Lord and what I was taught. I showed her by taking her through the Ten Commandments. I sensed that she was ready to be converted, but I didn't feel comfortable leaning over her husband to pray with her. Besides, he was continually trying to swing the subject back to basketball. Suddenly he got up and went to the restroom, so I leaned over and said, "Don't feel pressured, but if you would like to be born again now, I would be happy to pray with you." She took my hand and whispered, "Pray with me."

After we prayed, I gave her my recently acquired green Gideon New Testament with Psalms and Proverbs, something I didn't like parting with.

When a friend met me at the airport, I told him about the woman and how I'd given her my New Testament. He said that he just picked one up from his office when he left for the airport, and I was welcome to have it. As we got into his car, sitting next to the passenger seat was a green Gideon New Testament with Psalms and Proverbs. He said he had a choice of a number of colors besides green, and must have picked it up around the same time I was giving mine away.

On the flight back from Chicago to Los Angeles, I sat next to a woman who asked what I did for a living (the question was predictable, as I asked her first). I told her that I wrote Christian books. She said she didn't have a Christian background, and she seemed very open, so I took her through the Law. I am often asked how I do this without causing offense. I often use the Law in my testimony by saying something like, "I didn't realize that you can break the Ten Commandments *in spirit*. I hadn't committed adultery but the Bible says, 'Whoever looks at a woman to lust for her has already committed adultery with her in his heart.'"

On this occasion I opened up each Commandment gently and thoroughly. After half an hour of reasoning with her, she smiled and said, "Actually, I'm a Christian. I was born again a year ago, and I just wanted to hear what you have to say."

Although I hid it well, I was annoyed by her deception. After seven meetings that weekend, I wasn't happy about spending my time "preaching to the choir." She should have been thankful that she wasn't sitting by the emergency door.

Then she said something that made me sit up: "I've been having a guy come around a bit, *and letting him.*"

I said, "You what? *You have been having sex?*"

She said, "Yes."

"Do you know what the Bible calls that? It's called fornication, and no fornicator will enter the kingdom of God."

At that point she confessed that she had never heard the gospel the way I explained it. Her understanding of sin had been almost nonexistent. She agreed that her "conversion" was spurious. After seeing the serious nature of her transgressions, that her forgiveness necessitated the suffering death of the Messiah, she repented and yielded her life to the Savior.

She didn't have a Bible so I gave her my green Gideon New Testament with Psalms and Proverbs.

After the flight, while I was waiting for my luggage, I handed one of our "IQ Test" tracts to a man. When I pointed out that he, like nine out of ten others, had failed the test, he said, "Well, I'll be damned!"

I replied, "I certainly hope not. You need to repent and put your faith in Jesus Christ."

During the 1990s, 57,000 teenagers died on the roads of America. Most died because they weren't wearing a seat belt. Why? Because they never thought they would be involved in a car accident, let alone be killed in one. Masses die of alcohol or drug abuse. Why? Because they never thought they would be caught in its clutches and dragged to an untimely death. Even with the threat of AIDS hanging over this generation, they are still sexually promiscuous. Why? Because they think it will never happen to them. Death is far from the unregenerate human mind. A wise man once said that every man thinks every man is mortal, but himself. That is so true. Somehow we think death will pass over us. The thought that we could ever be damned couldn't be further from our minds.

It's as though the devil taunts unregenerate humanity by putting biblical truths in their mouths while, at the same time, blinding them to what they are saying: "as sure as hell," "I'll be damned," "hell will freeze over before that will happen," and "there will be hell to pay," to name just a few. But if you and I know the Lord, we know the truth of such fearful statements, and therefore cannot help pulling others into the lifeboat of the Savior.

A Roller Coaster Ride

Time is so short; spend it wisely, because the day will come when you will see that life is truly like a roller coaster ride. It begins with a feeling of excitement and anticipation. The whole of your life is before you. Suddenly you're over the hill and down you come screaming. The day will come when youth and energy will be but memories. If you are young, prove him wrong who said youth was wasted on the young. Burn with passion for God. I have heard from people who have suddenly gotten right with God and then looked back over a wasted life. It was not only wasted but was scarred with divorce, alcohol abuse, and all sorts of traps that the ungodly walk into. Save yourself some pain by keeping your heart free from sin.

If you are middle-aged, don't just retire and settle in. Do something for God while you are still able.

If you are no stranger to gray hair, use the wisdom you have gained to encourage others, and pray for laborers to reach this hopeless and lost generation.

All around us, people we haven't yet met are dying. On an average day, 84 people take their own lives and an estimated 1,838 attempt suicide. Every twenty-four hours more than 150,000 people are swallowed by death. Those strangers you pass in the streets, at school, in the store, and in your workplace have either *Life* or *Death* written across their foreheads; they either know God or they are lost. Don't see them as masses. See them as individuals.

In 1991, when a typhoon killed a massive 150,000 people in Bangladesh, I found it hard to move beyond the sympathetic stage. In a world where suffering, distress, and anguish are a part of daily living, it is easy to become almost wearied by another tragedy and more misery.

Look on those you pass on the streets as individuals held captive behind that dark door of death.

But then I picked up a news magazine and saw, to my horror, *individual* human bodies—men, women, and little children lying on a shore among the carcasses of cattle—and I found a remnant of compassion in this hardened heart of mine.

Don't thwart that potential energy of compassion by looking on people as multitudes. Make yourself look on those you pass on the streets as individuals held captive behind that dark door of death. Some will die of old age, some will die young, some will die through suicide, some will be murdered, some will die through drugs or alcohol, some will die by accident, some will die sick, and some will die healthy...but the fact is, they will all die! Time will prove that to be true. They sit in the shadow of death, waiting for its reality to fall upon them. Don't wait until tomorrow; seek and save that which is lost today.

May you and I as Christians get a grip on the fact that *each and every one of us is dying.* Our days are numbered. Pray earnestly with the psalmist, "So teach us to number our days, that we may gain a heart of wisdom." The wisest thing you can do with your numbered days is to win souls for God. If you don't know how to witness, ask for our book *Hell's Best Kept Secret;* it was written to help you be effective. Also see the back of this book for details about our School of Biblical Evangelism.

CHAPTER 17

THE EVOLUTION of STUPIDITY

F oolish" is an archaic word. "Stupid" is the modern equivalent, but its use is a bit harsh in today's word-sensitive society. Nowadays we don't call people stupid, because we have no tolerance for intolerance.

We have apparently come a long way since the days of condescension and bigotry. In fact, modern man thinks he has come a long way since the beginning of time, when we acted like animals toward each other. He doesn't really know when that "time" began, or even *how* we had our beginnings, but he's making concerted efforts to solve that dilemma. We spent $1.5 billion to build the Hubble Space Telescope and put it into orbit, and we spend another $230 million each year to keep it there to try to find our origins. Space may someday provide the answer. Meanwhile, "enlightened" man continues the search for our genesis... our humble human beginnings.

Our forefathers didn't have that dilemma. They knew when and where man came from. They simply believed that God made us "in the beginning," as the beginning of the Book of Beginnings (Genesis) so clearly states. The question then is, when did not believing the Book of Beginnings begin? What genius first decided that we shouldn't believe Genesis, and why did anyone believe him?

What genius first decided that we shouldn't believe Genesis, and why did anyone believe him?

Genesis-less-ness has left modern society with the dilemma of creating even more questions. What is the purpose of our existence? Where is the missing link? And which *did* come first, the chicken or the egg? Again, our forefathers knew the answers. They believed that God made us for Himself, that there is no missing link—because humans and animals were distinctly created by God, and each brought forth after its own kind—and that the first chicken came first, and the first egg came second.

But enlightened mankind rejects Genesis and hasn't the foggiest idea who laid what when. They don't know where they came from, what they're doing here, or where they are ultimately going. They do know that they are going to die, yet they don't know what causes death, what happens after death, or what to do about it.

They don't even know what makes a murderer murder. Experts have studied the profiles of multitudes of murderers so that we can better understand why they kill. With more than 600,000 murderers to study (just in the U.S. during 1970–2002), they should have come up with a clear and common profile. But they haven't. This is because they consider themselves too wise to believe the Book. It says that the common denominator among all murderers is their human nature, and that nature is inherently evil.

The Bible also says that the wisdom of this world is "foolishness" (Greek *moros:* "stupidity") with God. It also says that when men profess themselves to be wise, they become fools (stupid). I have seen this often, when atheists attempt to discredit those who believe the Bible by quoting history books that were written around the time of Christ. They blindly believe the historical recordings of men without a second thought.

The Bible calls anyone who denies the Creator a fool (stupid). Only dimwitted folks would say that a painting didn't have a painter, that a building didn't have a builder, and that creation had no Creator. These same folks often have blind faith in the theory of evolution, for which we have no irrefutable evidence. They believe a theory as though it were fact, and look down on people who have a trust in God, who has given us "many infallible proofs" (Acts 1:3). As Napoleon said, some people will believe anything "as long as it's not in the Bible." This is because it is a moral Book—from Genesis to Revelation, it accuses us of sin.

The epitome of human stupidity is the fact that God offers everlasting life to whoever wants it, and few seem to care. It appears that our stupidity began its "evolutionary" process in the species at the very moment sin entered the human race. However, its progress is stopped the moment God gives a sinner His Holy Spirit at the new birth. It is then that we receive a "sound mind" (2 Timothy 1:7). Thank God for

His intervening hand of grace, for without it we would still be sinking into the quicksand of this world's insanity: "For we ourselves were also once foolish [stupid], disobedient, deceived, serving various lusts and pleasures, living in malice and envy, hateful and hating one another" (Titus 3:3).

Powerful Rays

Have you ever driven a car toward the rising sun? Its glare is painful. It hinders you from seeing anything clearly. However, if you turn around and drive in the direction that the sun's rays are shining, everything you view will become clear. That's what happens at conversion. When a man's heart drives against the Law, the things of God frustrate and anger him. The Law's powerful rays spoil his outlook on sin. But the moment he turns from sin and places his faith in Jesus, he sees all things clearly. He knows the truth and the truth makes him free.

Have you ever seen the Law do its work? If not, then experiment with it. The next time you speak to an atheist who says, "I don't believe in God," just say, "Okay. Do you consider yourself to be a good person?" Learn the art of circumnavigating the intellect. When he says that he does, ask, "Have you ever told a lie?" If he has, ask, "What does that make you?" Have him confess that he is a "liar." Ask if he has ever stolen something. If he says no, say (in a friendly tone), "Come on...you've just admitted to me that you're a liar. Have you ever stolen anything in your whole life, even if it's small?" If he says yes, ask what that makes him—"a thief." Then say, "Jesus said, 'Whoever looks at a woman to lust for her has already committed adultery with her in his heart.' Have you ever looked with lust?" If he has, gently say, "What's your name?" ("John.") "John, by your own admission, you are a lying, thieving, adulterer at heart, and we've only looked at three of the Ten Commandments."

Take the same approach with a Mormon, a Muslim, an intellectual—anyone to whom you want to witness. Most Christians think that they have to bury their heads in the Koran or the Book of Mormon before they can witness effectively to those groups. Not so. Just bury your head in the Bible. God's Word is sufficient. When you lift up your head you should have your brain filled with these truths: "By the law is the knowledge of sin" (Romans 3:20); "I would not have known sin except through the law" (Romans 7:7); "The law was our schoolmaster to bring us unto Christ" (Galatians 3:24, KJV); and "The Law is good if one uses it lawfully" (1 Timothy 1:8).

After studying Scripture you should know that the area of battle isn't the sinner's intellect, it's his conscience. So if you just want to argue, stay in the intellect; but if you want to see sinners surrender to Jesus Christ, move the battle into the conscience, using the Law of God to bring the knowledge of sin.

It Was Nothing Serious

"My father died a few months ago." As I said those words to a man I had often encouraged to get right with God, the tone of our happy phone conversation suddenly changed. The man had never been openly angered by my words; in fact, he actually seemed to enjoy my company, laughing at most everything I said. I enjoyed his company, but at the same time felt frustrated that he was no spring chicken, and death could take him at any moment.

When I mentioned my dad's passing, the man soberly said, "I'm sorry."

I quickly replied, "Don't be. It was nothing serious." There was a deathly silence on the phone. "He was a Christian."

He then broke the silence with laughter, as though I had made some sort of joke. I continued, "I'm not kidding. Death has lost its sting. It is no big deal when a Christian dies."

Words can't express the joy (for want of a better word) I have in knowing that death has been destroyed by the Savior. I often pray that God would give me the wisdom to be able to make that message known, but at the same time I feel inadequate. I occasionally turn on a television and hear a well-known personality talk about dealing with life's dilemmas, and am amazed at his wisdom—and amazed at my lack of it.

Sinful men stand in moral judgment over a holy God, but He alone holds their breath in His hands.

I wouldn't have a clue how to answer the questions that are asked of him. Then I hear blasphemy slip out of his lips, and I am reminded that there is a wisdom of this world and there is a wisdom that comes from God. Anyone who blasphemes the name of the God who gave him the ability to think is a fool. He has real brain matter, but lacks brains in what really matters. The world's gurus can tell you everything about this life except how to keep it. How utterly tragic.

Late in 2002, Sir David Attenborough appeared on ABC's "60 Minutes." The famous, aging guru of evolution spoke candidly of his life's achievements, but his tone suddenly changed when the interviewer asked him if he had faith in God. It seemed that he saw a few evolutionary problems when it came to the hummingbird and the butterfly, but he deflected the issue by questioning the moral character of the Creator. He sited the African boy who was going blind because a worm was eating away within his eye. If God was the Maker of the worm, then He was a tyrant, guilty of a heinous crime against humanity.

The interviewer then asked the aging naturalist how he would like to die. Mr. Attenborough answered that it would be humiliating to die a slow and senile death, saying, "When I go, I hope to go quickly." He then smiled and added, "I almost said, 'God willing.'"

That is the bottom line. Sinful men may stand in moral judgment over a holy God, but He alone holds their breath in His hands.

What then should we say to those who question the ethics of God? The answer is to follow their line of reasoning until it takes them to the cross. The suffering child in Africa isn't the only evidence in "the case against God." What about the many American children who are dying of brain tumors? What about the hundreds of thousands of children throughout the world who are wasting away from starvation and various diseases? Who made the tornadoes that are ripping lives apart? Who created the killer hurricanes and the devastating earthquakes? Who withholds the rain, causing droughts that result in the death of multitudes? A thinking mind goes further than the worm, and asks the question, "Why is there disease, suffering, and death—is something wrong?" Something is indeed wrong. There is a case to be built, and if it is built correctly, it will reveal the true culprit.

As long as man is left in ignorance of the Law of God, he will lift himself up onto his throne of self-righteousness and accuse God of crimes against humanity. However, when the Law is allowed to do its wonderful work, it shows that we, not God, are the criminals, and that God is justified in all His deeds. When sin is seen in truth, one is left questioning the mercy of God, not His judgments.

CHAPTER 18

STARS of a DIFFERENT SORT

I crawled into bed and whispered to my wife, "I got beaten up tonight." As Sue stirred from her sleep, I mumbled, "...by a woman."

It wasn't the first woman to punch me with her fists. I have been slapped, hit in the mouth, slugged by a purse, abused, and chased by women. Once, while speaking to a crowd, I had the uplifting experience of being catapulted ten feet through the air by an angry Mormon. He ran at me from behind and hit me in my lower back with such force that I went from zero to 20 mph in a split second. Friends have been hit by flying objects just because they were sitting next to me after I preached. One member of our team (a good-

201

looking gentleman) was mistaken for me by an angry man who threatened to beat him up. A number of folk (usually drunk) have tried to hit me, but missed.

Only once have I felt that my life was in danger, and that was in Jerusalem in the late '90s. The previous night I had preached in Galilee, and the crowd had been so friendly that we decided that I would also preach in Jerusalem. However, from the moment I started to speak there was confusion in the air. After about fifteen minutes, an angry man began yelling at me and then spitting on me. A crowd even chased EZ, who was filming the event, to try to get his video camera (he thought he was going to die). He was able to slip the video to a friend, and when the crowd couldn't get hold of it, they left him alone.[5]

I had learned how to get out of hot situations, but this was one night when that wasn't going to happen.

Jerusalem wasn't the first spitting incident. I have been spat at and on a number of times by men, but it seems that members of the normally gentler sex are more capable of hitting their target, especially with their fists.

However, this night in Santa Monica had been a little more brutal. The 1991 L.A. riots had convinced me to move away from Stab Alley and find somewhere else to preach. I explored most of the beach areas before we found Santa Monica. I had been preaching there almost every Friday night for about three years and had learned how to get out of hot situations, but this was one night when that wasn't going to happen. An attractive woman, probably in her late twenties, had been offended by what I was saying. That didn't surprise me; it was normal to see anger in my listeners. I expected people to get upset when told that God not only informs us that murder, rape, adultery, lying, and stealing are morally wrong, but that He will punish those who do such things. After all, if we see fit to punish civil crimes through our court systems, how much more will God?

But this woman wasn't open to my reasoning. She lifted up her voice and used the "f" word twice, directed at me.

I looked at her and said, "Madam, could you watch your language? There are ladies present."

She snapped back, "I'm a lady!"

I managed a slight smile and said, "Madam, you may be a woman, but you are not a lady." Suddenly she ran at me like a bat out of Hades to confirm the truth of what I had just said.

As she began to punch me I thought, *This isn't the usual way a woman fights.* She wasn't scratching and slapping. She was placing punches like a trained prizefighter, and was able to get in six good blows before my team could pull her off. When she said, "Let me get my purse!" they made the mistake of letting her go, and she landed a powerful, perfectly placed punch to the kidney. I knew that a lot of the Hollywood elite live in Santa Monica, but my hope was to see "stars" of a different sort.

I was able to gather my thoughts and continue speaking to the crowd, which had more than doubled—something for which I was grateful.

It wasn't until the next morning that I gained empathy for prizefighters. I could hardly get out of bed. It took two weeks for the bruising to go away.

To be honest, I was a little disappointed that the bruises faded. I had preached open-air many times and didn't have even one scar to show for it. I had been hit on the forehead by coins (which did leave an impression on me), but even those marks disappeared quickly. Another open-air preacher, the apostle Paul, boasted that he bore in his body "the marks of the Lord Jesus." He received thirty-nine lashes five times for his faith, so his back must have looked like a crooked, freshly ploughed field. He was beaten and stoned to the point that the disciples thought he was dead, so my "persecution" was pretty petty compared to Paul's and the deep rivers of Christian blood that have flowed through the centuries. My angriest heckler was but a mild and friendly kitten compared to the ravaging mouths of hungry Roman lions.

One Line Please

The exciting thing about speaking in Santa Monica was that we were issued a permit. No longer would I be hassled by police. Many times while speaking I had been moved on by the law. While I don't mind a scar for the gospel's sake, I am not excited about being thrown into prison for my faith, so I had made it a habit of being particularly congenial to officers of the law. However, there was one time when I was eye to eye, nose to nose with a very angry officer, and I wasn't about to back down.

For more than three years I had given out gospel tracts at the local courts in our city. Each day, fifty to one hundred people from all walks of life lined up outside the courthouse to pay misdemeanor fines. The line was about sixty feet from my office window so I daily took advantage of the situation and handed out tracts. I was amazed at the reception. I would go to the front of the line and merely say, "Good morning. Make sure you get one of these, and read it thoroughly." Everyone would eagerly take one. I guess they thought it had something to do with their case...and it did. The day would come when they would face the Judge. But there was good news: I knew His Son, and knew how to get them acquitted.

Some days, instead of lining up, the crowd would gather in small groups to chat. That made my job more difficult, so I would go to the entrance of the courthouse and simply say, "One line please!" I was grateful to see that, within seconds, both lawyers and clients would stop their conversations and line up so that I could give them literature.

There was even a three-month period when I would go inside the lobby area to give the bored folks something to read while they waited. However, one day a security guard approached me and said, "You can't give those out in the waiting room anymore. Last night the city council gathered and passed an ordinance outlawing what you do." So I went back to the line.

Some months later, a police officer approached me and said, "You can't give those out on city property any longer. You have to give them out on the sidewalk."

I calmly replied, "This is public property. It is my First Amendment right to give them out."

The officer wasn't impressed. "People are leaving them in the courtrooms," he persisted. "I will arrest you for littering."

I gently said, "Arrest them. *They* are doing the littering."

He raised his voice as he repeated, "Do not give these out here! Go on the grass area and give them out there!"

"There's no one on the grass area," I argued. "I am an American citizen; this is my First Amendment right."

By this time he was breathing fire. He mumbled something unintelligible and stormed off.

Then they informed me that they had a new ordinance requiring that I stay ten feet back from the building.

I'm the Troublemaker

When I was in Israel, I had a little clash with our tour guide. As we headed for a site, he would announce whether it was traditional or authentic. Traditional usually meant that it was an area owned by the Catholic church that may have been where Jesus did some miracle. Authentic meant that there was no doubt about the site.

As we approached a certain area, the tour guide called out in a deep Middle Eastern accent, "Traditional site. No shorts."

I called back, "No shorts? It's over 90 degrees out there!"

"No shorts," he repeated. "When in Rome, do as the Romans do."

"The Romans wore miniskirts."

That's when he hollered, "Troublemaker!"—a label I wore for the whole tour.

About six months after the fuming police officer incident, I was in trouble again. I was led into the court lobby by a police officer, and duly told that I couldn't give out tracts to the people lined up outside the courthouse. When he said that it was county property I asked, "Isn't it public domain?" Rather than answer, he said he knew I'd been doing that for years, but that I had to stay on the sidewalk. He obviously felt uncomfortable, and encouraged me to speak with the sheriff. I said that I would like to, and asked for his name. It was Vern.

When I entered the sheriff's office, I spent some time talking with two receptionists. They loved the sleight-of-hand that I did for them (and the tracts I gave to them) while I waited to see the sheriff. Then they asked my name. When I told them, one widened her eyes and said, "Oh, they've been talking about you! You are the one they are trying to get rid of. *You want to talk to Vern?* You'd better have your shield on!" Three times over the next few minutes, she repeated, "You'd better have your shield on."

Suddenly Vern came out of his office. I was surprised to see that his gun was still in its holster. I had decided that when I introduced myself I wouldn't reach out to shake his hand. I didn't want to antagonize him further. I simply said, "Hello, Vern. My name is Ray Comfort. I am the trouble-maker who has been giving out literature for the last four years to people in line outside the courts. Is there a problem?"

He didn't go for his gun. Neither did he subdue me with Mace. To my surprise he reached out his hand and shook mine. Then he said, "No problem at all. It's your legal right. The court supervisor complained, but we explained that it was your legal right." He repeated, "No, it's your legal right."

I smiled and said, "Well, thank you. I appreciate your tell-ing me that. Good-bye." He smiled and I left, somewhat mys-tified, but still alive.

Perhaps You Are Being Stirred

I was sitting on a plane on the way to see my folks in New Zealand. I had done an atheist debate at a university the night before that had been moderated by an American missionary. By coincidence, he was on the same flight, so we sat together.

About ten minutes into the flight I showed him my new digital camera. It was compact and very high-tech, and he was duly impressed. As he looked at it, I heard a still, small voice say, "Give him the camera." This was no cheap throw-away camera—it was worth over $700—so I prayed, "Lord, if You want me to give him the camera, cause him to say, 'Give me your camera.'" I smiled to myself and relaxed with the thought, *That's the end of that. There's no way he's going to say, "Give me your camera."*

The missionary then looked at me and said, "Give me your camera...and I will take a picture of you and your folks when we arrive at the airport." Fifteen seconds later, he was the proud owner of a high-tech, compact digital camera.

Perhaps as you have been reading this book you have

heard a still, small voice saying, "You should do that." Maybe it's the thought that you should give out tracts, or verbally share your faith, or even preach in the open air. I dare you to put your mouth where your thoughts are. Say, "Lord, if that's You, and You want me to do this thing, make it obvious to me in some way." You may get a shock. If it is to preach open-air, the following are a few thoughts that may be of help to you.

Don't see the police as your enemy. I was in Colorado Springs wanting to preach open-air. The police had cordoned off a couple of blocks and it was an ideal place to preach. I approached four police officers and said, "Hi. My name is Ray. May I stand on a box and speak to these people?"

I have learned never to compete with cute kids, animals, or bagpipes at full throttle.

One of the officers said, "You will have to ask the supervisor. He's over there, but I don't think he will allow it."

I thanked the officer, then walked across to a police car and spoke to the supervisor through an open passenger-side window. I politely introduced myself and asked, "May I stand on a box and speak to these people?"

He simply said, "It's your First Amendment right." He then asked, "What are you going to say to them?"

When I answered, "I'm a Christian," he smiled and said, "Go for it!"

A little later, I walked over to a group of firefighters and began chatting with them. As I did so, I noticed that some were wearing kilts. When one of them mentioned that he played the bagpipes, I asked, "Why don't you go and get them and play 'Amazing Grace'? I want to speak to these people, and you can help me get a crowd."

I started to speak to the small group that had gathered. After I did some sleight-of-hand, the crowd began to get larger. When I jumped up on the box to speak, the crowd continued to grow. Things were humming.

Suddenly I heard a strange sound: it was the distinctive sound of bagpipes. They were in the distance, so thankfully the noise didn't disturb my preaching. Then I noticed that the noise was getting louder, and louder, and soon became deafening. It was my helpful friend! He had taken my suggestion to heart, and slowly walked into my crowd, neck veins bulging, making the sound of a hysterical, choking turkey with the volume of a jumbo jet at full throttle.

I stopped speaking, got off the soapbox, and let him take the stand. I have learned never to compete with cute kids, animals, or bagpipes at full throttle. So, be polite to the police, and think twice if you invite a bagpipe player to get you a crowd.

Another suggestion is to take a few extra dollars in your pocket. I was preaching to about a hundred people at Pasadena State University when a large, very loud young lady began shouting at almost everything I said.[6] She was so loud and so frequent that I would have preferred bagpipes. So I told the crowd, "If any of you guys would like to take this lady to lunch, I will pay for it!" One man immediately stepped forward, took my money, took the lady, and took off. I was happy, she was happy, and he seemed happy.

Kissed or Cussed: Facing Rejection

I was with a couple of friends at a restaurant in Los Angeles when my cell phone rang, so I moved outdoors from the bustle of the noise to take the call. As I was returning to my table, I passed a gospel tract to a woman who sat alone at a table. She looked at the tract, then to my surprise jumped up and kissed me on the cheek. I was delighted—not with the kiss, but with the woman's reaction to the tract.

A few weeks earlier I had been in an elevator in Florida, and I'd received a different response. A man to whom I had given a tract cussed at me, chewed me out, and spat what was left in little pieces onto the ground. I was devastated. I felt humiliated. I also felt as though I never wanted to give out another tract. Ever!

Rejection is a powerful blow to human pride. It cuts deep, like a burning arrow in the heart. It makes the most courageous of us want to withdraw in defeat. It is when that sharp arrow pierces the flesh that we need to think of the sinful woman of whom the Bible speaks in Luke 7:36–50.

Rejection is a powerful blow to human pride. It cuts deep, like a burning arrow in the heart.

She entered the house of a Pharisee, stood behind Jesus, and began to wash His feet with her tears. Perhaps she quietly approached the Master as He reclined at a table in typical Middle-Eastern fashion—on His side with His feet stretched out behind Him. As she listened to His gracious words, tears of contrition began to fall in great droplets onto His feet. We are told that (for some reason) the Pharisee didn't follow the custom of the day and wash the feet of his guests as they entered his home. As her tears mingled with the dust that was on Jesus' feet, she dropped to her knees and began to dry His feet with her hair. A woman's hair is her glory, but she so humbled herself that she forgot her natural vanity, and dried His dusty and wet feet with the locks of her hair.

Those who have heard the Savior's gracious words and seen their own sinful condition fall at the feet of Jesus and wash them in tears of contrition. They can be clothed with humility because they have been stripped of their pride and of this life's vanities. At the feet of the Savior, they understand that all that really matters is the approval of God. It is there that His will becomes their will. They too will want to have beautiful feet, shod with the preparation of the gospel of peace.

Then, when the world casts stones of rejection, we will look to the heavens and see Jesus standing at the right hand of God. When they nail our hands and feet to a cross of restraint, we still seek only the approval of God. When they offer the vinegar of bitter scorn so that fear causes our tongues to stick to our jaws, we will still speak, because we seek only the smile of God.

The next time you gaze at the moon, realize that its light is actually the result of solar radiation from a star so big that the earth fits into its volume a million times. This light was sent 93 million miles in a straight line traveling at 186,000 miles per second and hit dirt on the face of the moon. The light then was reflected toward the earth and traveled another 250,000 miles at the same speed, so that you could have soft light in the darkness of the night.

We are surrounded by many such miracles, but we don't give them a second thought. If we did, we would begin to comprehend that God is the Maker of this incredible creation that we so take for granted. When we see the unspeakable greatness of His power, we will recognize the importance of seeking His approval rather than that of the lowly dust He shaped into man by His miracle-working hand.

The moonlight will also remind us of the fact that even

though we are called "children of light," we don't have our own light. We merely reflect the light of Jesus, the Light of the World. One day He will reveal Himself in flaming fire. The pain of our rejection by this world pales compared to the unspeakable terror of the world's rejection by God.

The first time Jesus preached in his hometown His hearers were so wrath-filled that they tried to kill Him by throwing Him off a cliff (see Luke 4:29). But He didn't end His ministry simply because He was despised and rejected by men. Instead, He "committed Himself to Him who judges righteously." He looked to the smile of a holy God, rather than the frown of a sinful world.

So the next time you let your little light shine by preaching the gospel or giving out a tract, and a bucking bronco throws you for a loop, chews you up, and spits you onto the soil, remember the moonlight. Remember how it just reflects the brilliance of the sun. Then get up and find another horse, and get back into the saddle . . . while there is still time.

CHAPTER 19

LEFT BEHIND
at the AIRPORT

I t was May 2001. I had just watched the first of the *Left Behind* movie productions. The series of *Left Behind* books had been a runaway bestseller and the movie had followed in its steps, selling millions of copies. The movie was well-made, and I enjoyed seeing Kirk Cameron play the lead part. He had been in a number of major motion pictures and was so popular that during the seven-year production of the TV sitcom "Growing Pains" he received 10,000 fan letters each week. The movie had many wonderful references to God, the Bible, prayer, etc., and some salvation scenes showing the power of God's grace. But I would have loved to have seen the gospel even more fully presented. I know now that the producers had the same sentiment. In an evangelistic enterprise such as the making of a major motion picture, the challenge is ensuring that it is truly a movie and not just a thinly disguised sermon, since that would no doubt turn off the audience. However, I wondered how much further the boundary could be pushed. Could the gospel have been even more clearly presented without undue offense?

Some months before seeing the movie, my son-in-law EZ had spoken with the son of Jerry Jenkins, the co-author of the *Left Behind* series. The son told EZ that they were in-

We had seen Tim LaHaye standing at the Atlanta airport—left behind after missing his flight.

volved in a major *Left Behind* movie production starring Kirk Cameron. EZ introduced me and I took the opportunity to give him an audiotape of "Hell's Best Kept Secret" to pass on to his dad.

Just prior to that incident, my associate, Mark Spence, and I had attended the Christian Bookseller's Association (CBA) convention to promote my latest publication. We had seen Tim LaHaye, the other series co-author, standing at the Atlanta air-

port and decided to introduce ourselves. We soon learned that the famous author had been left behind after missing his flight.

I was surprised to find that he traveled alone and said, "I always travel with an associate. All it takes nowadays is for some woman to rub against you, accuse you of touching her inappropriately, and your ministry can been slurred." He smiled and said, "Son, when you are my age, no woman rubs up against you." We laughed, and I took the opportunity to get his address so I could send him a copy of "Hell's Best Kept Secret."

We didn't give him one personally because our supply of tapes had run out. Mark had given dozens to authors and other well-known Christian celebrities at the convention. I was proud of Mark's boldness. Instead of standing in line with hundreds of others, he would go to the front and say something like, "Excuse me. This is a tape you have just got to listen to," and then leave.

In a sense, the approach was easy for Mark because he so believed in the teaching. He had listened to the one-hour audiotape hundreds of times. He understood the importance of it and longed for others to see its great truths. He had even been able to get one into the hands of Kirk Cameron, who was at the CBA promoting *Left Behind: The Movie.* In Mark's usual bold fashion, he walked to the front of the line and said, "Excuse me, Kirk. You just have to listen to this teaching." Kirk was friendly, and graciously took the tape.

Celebrity Call

I get many phone calls, but a special sense of excitement gripped me with this one. I had been talking with one of the phone operators in our ministry when I heard my son Daniel say, "I recognized your voice." He then turned to me and said, "It's Kirk Cameron, from 'Growing Pains.'"

I quickly walked to my office, picked up the phone, and heard a distinctive voice say, "Hi, Ray. I'm Kirk Cameron. You may know me as Mike Seaver from the 'Growing Pains' television series."

He then went on to tell me that he had listened to "Hell's Best Kept Secret." While in his car on his way to a church to speak, he had slipped the tape into the player. What he heard was so radically different from what he was about to preach that it threw him for a loop. He had no choice but to share the message he had prepared, and ask God to forgive him. Then he listened to the tape again. And again.

Kirk was very enthusiastic during our thirty-minute conversation, and asked if I would be available to have lunch sometime.

After the call, I went to see what materials he had ordered. He had requested our "Excellence in Evangelism" 18-video series. This showed me that he was serious, so I picked up a copy of my book *Revival's Golden Key,* signed it, and placed the publication on top of the order.

The next day, my cell phone rang. It was Kirk. He had just watched the first video and said that he was devastated. He repeated that he wanted to meet with me for lunch, because he had so many questions about the teaching.

It was such an encouragement to know that a celebrity was genuine in his faith. Over the years many Hollywood stars have professed to be sincere, but time has revealed that their Christianity was just another acting job.

I'll Be Back

It was Monday around noon. I was a little nervous as I waited for a celebrity visitation. I don't think I would have been more excited if the President had been coming for lunch. Through the years in Santa Monica, I had rubbed shoulders with a few stars. Sort of. I had had a brief conversation with Arnold Schwarzenegger.[7] Very brief. When I asked him if he would like a tract, he gave a very resolute "No!" and walked off. James Cameron, director of the movie *Titanic,* asked for one of our "Titanic" gospel tracts, which didn't surprise me because the tract goes down well. Ricky Schroeder ("Silver Spoons" and "NYPD Blue") intently listened to me preach for twenty minutes. I had two encounters with Cathy Lee Crosby, and Dennis Weaver once listened to me speak for nearly an hour (he didn't have any choice, as he was sitting in the front row of a church at which I was the guest speaker).

When Kirk arrived, I went outside and greeted him as he

got out of his car. We then walked inside together and I introduced him to the staff. A few minutes later, Rachel, Mark, and I headed off to hobnob with a Hollywood bigwig. How cool.

I have often felt the pressure not to be my usual self when having lunch with pastors who were wanting me to speak at their churches. It's the pastor's chance to check me out before trusting me with his pulpit. Something in me would say, *Don't give out gospel tracts in the restaurant; be discreet. You will embarrass the pastor,* but I had learned to ignore it. I decided to ignore the thought on this occasion also.

As we entered the restaurant, I held up my wallet and showed my "ID" to the greeters. It is a computer-altered photo of me with my forehead stretched to about 14 inches. It looks ridiculous. It's the ultimate ice-breaker, and almost always gets laughs. It was once so appreciated by stressed airport staff that it was directly responsible for Mark and I being upgraded to business class.

Back in the restaurant, the staff packed around, partly because of the laughter at my photo and no doubt because they recognized Kirk Cameron. I took advantage of the situation and handed out gospel tracts to each person. When we sat at the table, I did some sleight-of-hand for the waiter and gave him one of our tracts, which he seemed to appreciate.

For the next three hours we sat in the restaurant and talked. During that time Kirk was asked if he would pose for photos with the staff, something he graciously did. He had many questions about what he had learned through the teaching. Fortunately, they were questions I had been asked before, and my answers seemed to satisfy him. Both Rachel and Mark had a good grip on the teaching and were also able to give valuable input to the conversation. As we left the restaurant, I visited the tables close to us and gave the occupants tracts.

After we got back to the ministry, it seemed that Kirk didn't want to leave. He not only stayed for another two hours, but he helped us load the UPS truck. He laughed at my jokes, and even at the dumb photos I had placed on the walls of our building. This man had a gift of discerning quality humor.

When he left I felt a sense of sadness. Still, it was a memory we would all cherish.

Rocked Out of My Chair

The next day I received the following e-mail:

> Ray,
> For weeks, I had been looking forward to meeting with you, hoping to find a man of God. Instead I found a lunatic. Just kidding.
> I was so fired up after leaving your place! Your teachings on the Law and grace have made more sense to me than anyone else's, and I am so thankful for what God is doing...I believe I was robbed of the deep pain of seeing the depth of my sinfulness, of experiencing the exceeding joy and gratitude that comes from the cross, because I was convinced of God's love before I was convinced of my sin. I didn't see the big problem, but by faith believed I was a sinner (many worse than me, but nevertheless a sinner), and repented of my "general sinful, selfish attitude." I had never opened up the Ten Commandments and looked deep into the well of my sinful heart. I never imagined that God was actually angry with me at a certain point because of my sin. Because of "grace," I kind of skipped over that part and was just thankful that He loved me and had promised me eternal life.
> While I think I was saved thirteen years ago, I was rocked out of my chair last night, on my knees confess-

ing the *specific* sins that have plagued my heart that were never uncovered before. I think my knowledge of the "new covenant" and "under grace, not Law" kept me from ever examining my heart by the light of the Ten Commandments. The new weight of my sin is causing more pain in me...wounding my ego, and showing me how much more Jesus had to pay to set me free. Oh, the wonderful cross!!!!

Over the next few months it became common to hear one of the staff buzz me and say, "It's Kirk." In fact it became quite normal to hear from him every day, and each call was as exciting as the first. We both decided that God had drawn us together and knit our hearts for a reason.

Cloud on the Horizon

Kirk mentioned that he and his wife, Chelsea, were considering doing another *Left Behind* movie, but there were problems with the first script they were sent. (Chelsea played flight attendant Hattie Durham.) The next day he called to say, "They've sent me another script. It is really good—I mean *really* good. I will e-mail this one to you. Let me know what you think."

I later learned that Cloud Ten Pictures, the Christian film studio producing the movie, made a deal with their production partner that allowed them to replace the original script with a more evangelistic one. What I had in my hands was the first draft of this transformed script.

I read the entire script in two hours. It was good. The story line held my attention, and as I read it I marked where I thought it could use additional gospel input. I went over it with Mark, then called Kirk. As I did so, I could hardly believe what we were doing. Only a year earlier I was watching the first *Left Behind* movie and imagining how the gospel could be further incorporated. Now I not only had in hand the script of perhaps the most anticipated prophecy movie ever, but I was suggesting revisions.

Although I didn't know it at the time, what we were doing was not just unorthodox, but was an attempt at the impossible. The scriptwriters write the script. That's their job. Stars are paid big bucks to star in the movie; that's their job.

What we were doing was not just unorthodox, but was an attempt at the impossible.

No matter how big the name, they are rarely given permission to rewrite major portions of the script.

Nevertheless, we spent hours on the phone rewriting certain scenes, and acting them out to see if they sounded right. As I listened to Kirk give his thoughts, I was amazed at his maturity and understanding of the Scriptures. He wasn't just some Hollywood poster-boy who had simply added Jesus to his life, but a godly man and a gifted Bible teacher.

The next day Kirk called to inform me that he and Chelsea were seriously thinking of turning down their parts in the movie. He said that there were other difficulties beside the needed script changes. Filming was scheduled to start in two weeks, but contracts hadn't yet been signed. He wasn't even sure who the other stars would be. If he played opposite bad actors, it could damage his reputation. He seemed to have made up his mind, and tried to lessen any disappointment on my part by saying that he would send the producers the suggested script changes.

Such a Time as This

The following day I sent Kirk an e-mail:

Kirk,

It's early Sunday morning. I have been lying awake since 4:00 a.m. horrified at the thought of you not doing the movie. We've got a good solid friendship, so I feel at liberty to share my heart.

Let's pull back and see what an opportunity is being given to you. When someone takes a tract from me, I am thrilled. Here is a possibility that a human may read the Word of God, and may sometime in the future come to a place of true repentance and find *everlasting life!* When I pour my heart out (preaching open-air) at Santa Monica and become subject to hatred, insults, and filthy language (like you wouldn't believe), in the back of my mind I am thinking that perhaps, among the hearers, there is someone who is listening and may find everlasting life. My great confidence is that I am doing what I have been commanded to, and that God's Word cannot return void.

Through this movie you have an unprecedented opportunity to preach this incredible gospel (the whole counsel of God) to millions. Billy Graham may have reached one or two million in a year, but you can reach ten, perhaps twenty, million or more through one movie. If I were you, I would apply Paul's attitude to this situation. Here it is:

"If I preach the gospel, I have nothing to boast of, for necessity is laid upon me; yes, woe is me if I do not preach the gospel! For if I do this willingly, I have a reward; but if against my will, I have been entrusted with a stewardship. What is my reward then? That when I preach the gospel, I may present the gospel of Christ without charge, that I may not abuse my authority in the gospel. For though I am free from all men, I have made myself a servant to all, that I might win the more;

...I have become all things to all men, that I might by all means save some" (1 Corinthians 9:16–22).

Kirk, if I were you, I wouldn't look at this as an actor, but as a preacher. As an actor, you should be concerned about your reputation...but as a preacher of the gospel you can make yourself of no reputation.

Name one other human in history who has had the opportunity you are being offered. Perhaps you were born for such a time as this...

With all that said, whatever you decide is your business, and I will respect that. This is because our friendship comes a close second to the cause of the gospel. I can't tell you what a joy it is to be your friend. I thank God for bringing you into my life.

Ray

He sent me an immediate reply. It simply said, "Praying hard." Although I thought it may jeopardize a very valuable friendship, I sent another e-mail:

Kirk,

A group of firefighters arrive at a building that is on fire. Dozens of people trapped on the sixth floor are screaming for help. Terrified onlookers sigh with relief when the firefighters arrive, but become frustrated that they aren't getting out of their vehicle. They find that the head firefighter is calling headquarters to see if he should attempt to rescue the people.

There are some things a firefighter doesn't need to call headquarters about, and there are some things we need not even ask God about, because of the clear mandate He has given us. We have been told to "Go into all the world and preach the gospel to every creature," and to "Preach the Word! Be ready in season and out of season." When Jesus looked upon the multitude, there is no record that He sought the Father in prayer to see if He should feed them. There is no record that Peter prayed about whether he should preach to the unsaved on the Day of Pentecost. God knows that if He offered me what He has offered you, the only prayer I would pray is, "Thank you, Lord. What an opportunity; what an honor! For to me, to live is Christ" (the Living Bible says, "For to me, living means opportunities for Christ").

You have told me that if you could just wait for a door to open in the movie industry, instead of preaching to thousands (as you do now), you could preach to millions. It's here, Kirk. This is your opportunity. Perhaps it came quicker than you thought … it just didn't come in the fancy Hollywood wrapper.

Spurgeon said something like, "If God has called you to be a missionary, don't shrink down to be

Spurgeon said something like, "If God has called you to be a missionary, don't shrink down to be a king." If God has called you to be a preacher, don't shrink down to be Hollywood's greatest star. Stars fade so quickly. Despite reruns, this generation doesn't even know who Jimmy Stewart and Marlon Brando are. If the Lord tarries, in fifty years time they won't even know who Tom Cruise is, or his movies will be so low-tech they will be a joke.

How long do we have? Look at what's happening in Israel. These are the last moments of time. Seize the moment, Kirk. The script is excellent, and you have the opportunity to help lock in the gospel presentation. What more could you want?

Ray

The next day Kirk called and said that he had received the second e-mail. He then laughed in a now familiar way, and sincerely thanked me for being forthright with him. He had decided to do the movie.

The next step was to talk with Peter and Paul Lalonde, who run Cloud Ten Pictures, and see if they'd be open to letting us work with them on the script—something that is just not done in the film industry.

CHAPTER 20

WHY *the* CHANGES?

To illustrate why we felt the changes to the script were necessary, let's look for a moment at a scene from the first *Left Behind* movie. One of the most thought-provoking incidents in the movie was the fact that a pastor named Bruce Barnes was left behind. It seems strange that that happened. He did believe in God. He no doubt had "invited Jesus into his heart." He never missed a Sunday service. He read his Bible. He prayed. He preached. He even led others in prayers of salvation. He baptized believers. The man was a pastor! He seemed to be a model Christian, *yet he was left behind.* Why?

Jesus gives us the answer in Matthew 7:21–23. He warned that *many* would consider themselves Christians and yet not be saved. Jesus said, "Not everyone who says to Me, 'Lord, Lord,' shall enter the kingdom of heaven...Many will say to

Me in that day, 'Lord, Lord, have we not prophesied in Your name, cast out demons in Your name, and done many wonders in Your name?' And then I will declare to them, 'I never knew you; depart from Me, you who practice lawlessness.'" Wow. Look at how committed people can be and still not make it to heaven:

- They called Jesus "Lord."

- They prophesied in His name.

- They cast out demons.

- They did many "wonders" in His name.

These people are more spiritual than most of us, and yet they will be rejected by the One they call "Lord." How can we ensure that we will not be one of those who will be rejected by Jesus in that day? There is a way to know.

The key is in verse 23. Jesus said to them, "Depart from Me, you who practice *lawlessness.*" He is speaking here of the Moral Law—the Ten Commandments. The way to make sure of our salvation, then, is to look seriously at the Ten Commandments and see for ourselves how we will do on the Day of Judgment. No doubt you are like me and the rest of humanity, and you will be guilty. Do you think guilty sinners will go to heaven or hell? Tragically, many believe they will go to heaven; they think that God is "good" and that He will therefore overlook their sins. Try that in a court of law. Imagine someone has committed rape and murder. The judge says, "You are guilty. Do you have anything to say before I pass sentence?" and he says, "Judge, I believe that you are a good man, and therefore you will just let me go." The judge would probably say, "I *am* a good man, and it's because of my goodness that I will see to it that you are punished!" The truth is that if God gives the criminal justice, he's not headed for heaven, but for hell. The very thing that many are hoping will save them on the Day of Judgment is the very thing that will condemn them. If God is "good," He must by nature punish murderers, rapists, thieves, liars, fornicators, adulterers, etc. Be sure of it, He will punish sin wherever it is found.

We must therefore take the time to do what the Bible says: "Examine yourself to see whether you are in the faith" (2 Corinthians 13:5). Many won't do this until the Day of Judgment, when the Commandments seek them out. In the meantime, they tell fibs and white lies, take things that belong to others, harbor bitterness in their hearts, covet the things of others, and have a wandering eye when it comes to the opposite sex. They don't see sin as being very sinful. However, God sees them as lying, thieving, hateful, greedy, adulterers at heart. That's why it is so important for us to see ourselves in truth, under the light of God's Law. Otherwise, we make the fatal mistake of thinking that God's

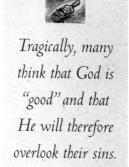

Tragically, many think that God is "good" and that He will therefore overlook their sins.

standards are the same as ours, and that we have nothing to be concerned about. That is the ultimate deception. Like Kirk, we will only appreciate the depth of God's love and forgiveness when we understand how deeply we have sinned against Him.

Had the pastor examined himself in the mirror of God's holy Law, he would have seen himself in truth and recognized his need for cleansing.

When we reason with people using the Law of God (the Ten Commandments), it has the power to convince them of their danger. It shows them that they need a Savior. This was the key to the success of all the great preachers God has used down through the centuries, and this is what was missing both in the script and in the modern gospel.

Kirk and I wondered if Cloud Ten would be willing to incorporate this into their revised, already good script. After all, it was their money on the line. Although they were committed to the gospel, using the Law in evangelism is a new concept to many. We held our breath as Kirk approached them with our suggested additions and ideas. With all that was going on, I wondered how he would sleep that night.

This Is Impossible

"Hey, Ray. It's Kirk. I'm calling from Toronto. I've just spent forty-five minutes with one of the producers explaining the use of the Law in evangelism, *and he loves it!* I went through every illustration I know and he has seen its importance. This is wonderful!"

Kirk was very excited. I was too, because he had told me that outside of his initial conversion experience, he hadn't seen God do much in his life in the area of the supernatural. Now it seemed that he was beginning to see something miraculous take place.

I had seen God do many wonderful things in my thirty years as a Christian. One experience in particular helped me to know that nothing is impossible when it comes to God.

I regularly surf atheist web sites on the Internet. It was during one of these "surfing" days that I came up on the dry shores of the American Atheists, Inc. web site. I decided to ask them if they would allow me to speak at one of their conventions. After all, they were undoubtedly convinced that no one could prove the existence of God, and that if I were allowed to speak I would simply say that we must have "faith" to believe in God. That was an argument they could shoot down in flames, and therefore they might (it was a long shot), on that basis, allow me to speak.

I carefully formulated an e-mail asking if they would consider me as a guest speaker at their national convention. I explained that I had spoken extensively on the subject of atheism at Yale and other prestigious learning institutions. I had written a booklet called "The Atheist Test" that had sold over a million copies, as well as a book titled *God Doesn't Believe in Atheists: Proof That the Atheist Doesn't Exist*.

They graciously declined my offer, which I took as a compliment, although I was disappointed. I had hoped that God would somehow do a miracle and open the door. On reflection, I realized I was actually asking for the impossible. Imagine—an atheistic organization having a preacher as a guest speaker! How naïve.

Who's the Chicken?

Sometime later I found myself crossing swords with Ron Barrier (the spokesperson for American Atheists, Inc.) via e-mail. At one point he asked if I would have the courage to face him in a debate at their national convention in Orlando, Florida. I told him that I would be delighted, and said that I would even pay my own airfare from Los Angeles to Florida.

He then read *God Doesn't Believe in Atheists* and quickly withdrew the offer. Shortly after that incident, a number of other atheists began writing to me, and when one called me a "chicken," I told him that it was Ron Barrier who deserved that title because he had "chickened" out of a debate. They didn't believe me, so I found his finger-lickin' good e-mail and forwarded it to them. They roasted him to a point where he admitted to it, renewed the offer, and then sweetened the pot by flying me at their expense from Los Angeles to Florida to debate at their 2001 national convention.

My video production manager, Ron Meade, went with

me. They put us in a classy hotel and gave us a fruit basket with a welcome card. It was a wonderful experience. The debate was broadcast live on their web site, and they gave us permission to videotape it.[8]

Ron Barrier and I cosigned my book together for their library, and we even hugged after the debate. It was like a dream. What I had hoped for was ridiculous, bizarre, and ludicrous. It was impossible—but with God *nothing* shall be impossible.

One-Way Ticket Home

Because of this, and other experiences, I felt we could believe that God could do anything. Kirk called to tell me that he discovered the two other producers lived a couple of hours away. He decided to rent a car and visit them because production was due to start in two days. If he didn't talk to them immediately, it would be too late to make any changes.

About two hours later Kirk was on the other end of the line again, but this time his voice was different. He said, "I rented a car and was about to leave when I found out that the producers aren't even home. Now I have been given the latest script, Ray, and there are big problems with it. It's not the moviemaker's fault—we may just be out of time. What we were attempting to do was impossible anyway. I don't think we can get this done. I am considering getting a one-way ticket home."

We spent the next twenty minutes talking and came to the conclusion that there was no miracle without a lion's den. There was no resurrection without a body. There was no opening of the Red Sea without Pharaoh at the heels of Israel. Obviously there is no movie without a good script, but we decided to drop any "buts" and "what ifs," and trust God for a miracle. We were in for a surprise.

This Is a Miracle!

The next day Kirk asked me to send him quality quotations from great preachers of the past, commending the use of the Law in evangelism, as he was going to try to pull a meeting together. This is what I sent him:

> Kirk, here are the quotes:
>
> John Newton (wrote "Amazing Grace"): "Ignorance of the nature and design of the Law is at the bottom of most religious mistakes."
>
> Charles Spurgeon (the Prince of Preachers): "I do not believe that any man can preach the gospel who does not preach the Law...Lower the Law and you dim the light by which man perceives his guilt; this is a very serious loss to the sinner rather than a gain; for it lessens the likelihood of his conviction and conversion. I say you have deprived the gospel of its ablest auxiliary [most powerful weapon] when you have set aside the Law. You have taken away from it the schoolmaster that is to bring men to Christ...They will never accept grace till they tremble before a just and holy Law. Therefore the Law serves a most necessary purpose, and it must not be removed from its place."
>
> Jonathan Edwards (who preached the famous "Sinners in the Hands of an Angry God"): "The only way we can know whether we are sinning is by knowing His Moral Law."
>
> George Whitefield: "First, then, before you can speak peace to your hearts, you must be made to see, made to feel, made to weep over, made to bewail, your actual transgressions against the Law of God."
>
> John Wesley: "It is the ordinary method of the Spirit of God to convict sinners by the Law. It is this which, being set home on the conscience, generally breaks the

rocks in pieces. It is more especially this part of the Word of God which is quick and powerful, full of life and energy and sharper than any two-edged sword."

Martin Luther: "The first duty of the gospel preacher is to declare God's Law and show the nature of sin."

C. S. Lewis: "When we merely say that we are bad, the 'wrath' of God seems a barbarous doctrine; as soon as we perceive our bad-ness, it appears inevitable, a mere corollary from God's goodness…"

Charles Finney: "Evermore the Law must prepare the way for the gospel. To overlook this in instructing souls is almost certain to result in false hope, the introduction of a false standard of Christian experience, and to fill the Church with false converts… Time will make this plain."

John Bunyan (author of *Pilgrim's Progress*): "The man who does not know the nature of the Law, cannot know the nature of sin."

Kirk responded with a phone call to thank me for the quotes. I was pleased to hear the usual optimism in his voice as he told me that he was about to meet with the director and producers. He said, "Pray that God does a miracle. Pray hard."

Over the next several hours, I prayed. I prayed hard, like you would pray for a loved one who was in serious surgery.

Blow by Blow

Four hours later the phone rang. It was Kirk. I told him that I had said to Sue that either he was having a good, long meeting with the producers, or he was lying on the floor, discouraged and dejected, and it took him four hours to crawl to the phone.

He then held the phone away from his mouth and hollered, "Thank you, Lord!" He was ecstatic, and gave me a blow-by-blow account of what happened.

Before the meeting he asked me if I thought he should show them a video. It was forty-five minutes of Kirk preaching major portions of "Hell's Best Kept Secret" at a huge church in San Diego. He delivered it with such God-given ability that the congregation gave him a standing ovation.[9]

We decided that it was important to show the executives the video, as it would not only fully explain why the script additions were needed, but it would show them that Kirk was a sincere Christian and not just a Hollywood flake.

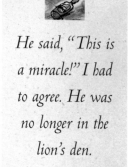

He said, "This is a miracle!" I had to agree. He was no longer in the lion's den.

So he spoke his piece, and then switched on the video. He paced around the room for the next forty-five minutes, thinking they were bored. But by the end of the video, they were completely convinced that the additional changes were needed, despite the impossible deadlines they were under—and remember that they had already changed the entire script just a few weeks before filming started. Kirk was thrilled to find that the producers had the same vision and were very open to the input. He said, "This is a miracle!" I had to agree. He was no longer in the lion's den.

CHAPTER 21

WELL-OILED MACHINE

Things were moving so fast that it made our heads spin. It was late at night and Mark and I were sitting in the Los Angeles airport, waiting to take off on a red-eye flight to Toronto. Kirk had invited me to join him on the set. The last-minute ticket was very expensive, so I told Mark that he was welcome to join me if he could use his frequent flyer miles. However, the airline informed him that a 24-hour wait was required before mileage could be used. Mark thought for a moment, then said, "I am the associate of an author who has been working with Kirk Cameron on a movie script, and he wants us on the set." Suddenly the operator's demeanor changed. "Kirk Cameron! My husband used to be jealous because I had a crush on him. I'll see what I can do." Within minutes, Mark and I were booked to fly together to Toronto.

The next evening we joined Kirk on the *Left Behind* set. Nearly one hundred people milled back and forth, each with a specific set of duties. As Kirk's guests, we were treated like royalty. We were given food and drinks, and I was provided with earphones so I could hear the actors clearly, and even my own "director's chair." It was amazing to see the precision with which everything worked. Like a well-oiled machine, the moment the director called "Cut!" dozens of people moved in with their particular expertise.

It is unwise to give a sinner (who is apologizing to God for sinning against Him) a "form" prayer.

The set looked like the inside of a smoke-filled hospital room. It was actually a makeshift hospital in which lay the wounded and dying. The fake "smoke" was harmless, and gave atmosphere to the shoot.

In one bed lay a badly burned fireman. Amazingly, just a few days earlier Kirk and I had worked on this scene. The original script had the fireman coming to God through the usual "sinner's prayer." I said that I wasn't a big fan of that method. My reasoning was that if a man has committed adultery and his wife is willing to take him back, should I have to give him a handwritten letter of apology to read to her? No. She isn't interested in his words. All she wants to know is if he is truly sorry for what he has done. That's why I think it is unwise to give a sinner (who is apologizing to God for sinning against Him) a "form" prayer. God isn't interested in his words, as much as He is interested in the sorrow of his heart.

So we proposed the following scene. The firefighter whispered, "I'm ready..." Chloe leaned forward to hear what the man was saying. He said, "I'm ready...for God..." She replied, "Then tell Him."

The burn victim's voice seemed to reveal that he had more pain in his soul than in his body. He immediately whispered, "Oh, God...I'm sorry. I'm sorry for sinning against You. Thank You, Jesus, that You died for me. I give You... my...life." Then he breathed his last breath. It was a very moving scene.

The next day Mark and I went to a local park to preach open-air during the lunch hour, but there were only a few small groups of people rather than the crowds we had expected. When a group of high school kids arrived, I approached them with tracts, my stupid picture, and some sleight-of-hand. They loved it, took the tracts, and listened to every word I said. Mark recorded the encounter on video and that night we sat down with Kirk and viewed it together. He was free the next day, so we planned to go somewhere and preach open-air.

It rained...all day. Kirk wasn't due on the set until 8:00 that night, so we spent almost the entire time in our hotel room enjoying each other's company and talking about the amazing experience of working on *Left Behind II*. It was incredible. Our time of fellowship was interrupted only briefly while Kirk went through his lines with another cast member.

That night on the set I spoke with Jenny, who was in charge of wardrobe. She was in her early forties and was very friendly. She was intensely interested in the subject of God, so I shared a few thoughts between takes. When we parted that evening, I told her that the next day we could pick up where we left off. She seemed interested in doing that.

All That Garbage!

The following day I mentioned to Jenny about the small part I had played in revising the script. I explained that Kirk had read one of my books and seen the importance of incorporating certain principles into the movie. I told her that it was those very principles that made the Christian message make sense. She was deeply interested, so I took her through a few of the Ten Commandments. She had violated each of them, and saw that if she stood before God on the Day of Judgment, she would be in big trouble. When I stated that that was the reason Jesus died on the cross, she widened her eyes and replied, "That's something I never understood…"

She now understood the Law, and therefore the gospel was no longer a foolish message to her.

As I explained that she had broken the Law and that Jesus had paid her fine, it was as though a light went on in her head. She now understood the Law, and therefore the gospel was no longer a foolish message to her.

I hoped that we could achieve the same result with the movie, so I was particularly interested in the scene they were about to shoot. This was a sequence we had spent hours on.

Chris burst out of the church. An hour or so earlier, Ray [and Buck, played by Kirk] had welcomed him into the meeting. Chris wasn't a Christian but he had reluctantly agreed to come. However, the pastor's mention of the Antichrist, sin, and judgment had made him fume to a point of walking out of the meeting.

He angrily burst through the doors and out into the night. Ray followed hard on his heels and asked why he was so upset. Chris stopped in the semidarkness of the churchyard and spat out, "I can't sit there and listen to that garbage! 'Save us from sin, Nicholae's the Antichrist'—come on. That's the problem with you people.

You think everyone is 'bad.' Let me tell you something. There are a lot of good people in this world. Including me."

Suddenly a familiar voice asked, "According to whose standards—yours or God's?" It was Buck. He had followed Ray and Chris out of the church.

Chris was taken aback with that question, and responded, "What?"

"You're a good person? Do you think you've kept the Ten Commandments?"

Chris said, "Yeah, pretty much. I'm not perfect, but I've never killed anybody."

"Have you ever lied?"

"Well, yeah. Who hasn't?"

"What does that make you?"

Chris retorted sarcastically, "Human."

"Come on, be honest. If you murder someone, it makes you a murderer. If you've lied, what does it make you?"

"Okay, a liar."

"Have you ever stolen anything? Even if it's something small?"

Chris winces a little as he says, "No. Well...yeah. Once."

"So what does that make you?"

Chris was beginning to get a little uncomfortable as he answered, "A thief."

"This is the one that got me. Jesus said that even if you look at a woman with lust in your heart, you've already committed adultery."

Chris laughed nervously. "Yep, guilty."

"Chris, by your own admission, you're a lying thief and an adulterer at heart, and that's only three of the Ten Commandments. If God judges you by those standards, will you be innocent or guilty?"

"I guess I'd be guilty."

"Chris, that's the point. When we stand before God, we're all guilty. If you don't get your heart right with God before that Day, you'll get the punishment you deserve. But that's not what God wants."

"What am I supposed to do? Get religious?"

Suddenly Ray butted in. "No, that's what we're trying to tell you. Jesus took the punishment for your sins upon Himself when He died on the cross. God did that so you wouldn't have to go to hell. That's how much God loves you. Eternal life is a gift. You don't have to do anything 'religious.'"

What happened to Chris after that? To find out ... you will have to see the movie.

CHAPTER 22

WINNING
the BATTLE

As the three of us were having breakfast in the hotel in Toronto, Kirk mentioned, "I really want to use this platform God's given me to further the gospel." I told him that I am forced to use humor to break the ice with strangers so that I can share with them, but his celebrity gives him instant credibility even with strangers.

I then told him that I battle with fear every time I give anyone a tract. He was skeptical. Like most people who know of my "reputation," he mistakenly thought that I didn't have any fear. He admitted that he cringed with embarrassment the first time he went to a restaurant with me. He intentionally distanced himself from me over the next few weeks, but felt that God wanted him to also reach out to the lost, and even hand out a tract here and there. As time passed, he became convinced that gospel tracts were a legitimate means of evangelism. His reasoning was that if he was sitting in a restaurant and he really cared about the fate of unsaved people, he would try to reach them in some way. He surmised that perhaps he would grab a napkin and write, "Please take the time to read the Bible—consider your eternal salvation," fold it and pass it to a stranger as he left. That's basically what a tract is—a well-written gospel message on a classy napkin.

Over breakfast each of us shared our fears. We talked out how difficult it was to actually give a tract to someone due to the fear of being rejected. If someone took the tract, we would think, *Please don't open this until I leave!* We discussed our concerns that someone would take a tract and ask, "What is it?"

Suddenly, to the horror of the three of us, one of the men picked up a tract and asked, "What is this?"

Kirk looked at me and said, "Take for instance those four businessmen sitting at the next table. How would you approach them?"

As we finished our breakfast, he took four of our "Something to Think About" tracts from his pocket and said, "Let me see how you do this." I picked up the tracts, walked a few paces to the other table and said, "Hello, gentlemen. Was the food okay?" They replied that it was great, and as they did so I said, "Here's something you may like to read when you have a moment." I placed the tracts on the table in front of them.

They were very congenial, and immediately looked at Kirk and asked him why his face was so familiar. I quickly introduced him and Mark. This was great—Kirk's celebrity was furthering our cause. The problem was, the men were flipping through the booklet as they talked. I felt like saying, "Put that down. Read it when we've gone. I want to wind up this conversation and make a quick getaway."

Suddenly, to the horror of the three of us, one of the men picked up a tract and asked, "What is this?" I quickly changed the subject by doing a sleight-of-hand routine, which greatly impressed them. Then, as we began to make our escape, the man asked again, "What is this?" This time there was no dodging the question. I reluctantly replied, "Oh, it's just a little gospel tract." The demeanor of all four men suddenly changed. The laughter fizzled, and they mumbled, "Oh...okay."

As we walked through the restaurant, Kirk led the way, feeling like the perpetrator of a bait-and-switch operation. I almost stepped on his heels as I whispered from behind, "Walk faster!" Then we started laughing, and the three of us broke into a run as we exited the restaurant.

It was hard to believe, but almost everything we had talked about during breakfast happened in the minute or two that we spoke to the businessmen. Afterwards we had a frank discussion on why we wanted to get away. None of us were ashamed of the gospel, so why should we want to run?

Three answers come to mind. We were in a classy restaurant with other folks sitting at nearby tables, and if we had engaged in a conversation and there had been contention from the businessmen, we would have been (understandably) embarrassed. I was with two friends and if I had humiliated myself in some way, it would have been compounded by them witnessing it. And of course, our battle wasn't against flesh and blood. There were spiritual forces at work.

If you are a Christian, shouldn't you be using tracts to reach out to the unsaved? We can help you. Kirk and I have written tracts that are almost fun to give out (you can see them at www.livingwaters.com). Whatever you do, don't make the mistake of sitting in the fire engine while people are burning to death. Each of us has a moral obligation to rescue the lost, with the help of God.

Battle Strategies

Here are a few strategies to help in the battle if you fear rejection. Choose an environment in which it will be less likely for these fears to be realized. Start with someplace that, if worst comes to worst, will be more private than public. You may want to begin by yourself without the company of friends. Perhaps you could just leave a tract in an elevator or in a shopping cart, or hand out tracts as you leave a supermarket or restaurant parking lot.

Choose a tract that you feel comfortable with. It may be one of ours that has plenty of "getaway time" ("101 of the World's Best One-Liners"), or one that makes it abundantly clear to people what you are giving them ("Are You Good Enough to Go to Heaven?").

The bold approach may be easier than the undercover approach because at least there is no fear of being "discovered." Give a tract to a restaurant waiter or someone behind a counter as you are leaving a store. Be determined to handle rejection if it does come. If someone refuses to take the tract, try not to let that discourage you. After giving out hundreds of thousands, my greatest battle is with the devastation of having just one person say, "No, thank you!"—especially if I'm in the company of other people.

Mentally prepare your mind to be flooded with different fears. Learn to ignore them, or deal with them by quoting the Word of God—such as, "I can do all things through Christ who strengthens me" (Philippians 4:13). Prepare yourself to make a quick getaway from the battle scene if you wish. However, never forget the fact that you *are* in a battle. It is what the Bible calls the "good fight of faith," exhorting us to "fight." It is called "good" because there is no more worthy cause than the battle for the souls of men and women. So, make heaven rejoice.

Spiritual Growing Pains

The same day Mark and I arrived back in Los Angeles, Kirk called and was ecstatic. He had previously mentioned that he was tempted to share tracts with some film extras as they sat in the church waiting for a shoot, but he hadn't made the move. I suggested that if he gave a dead cockroach to each of the extras, they would take it home and put it in a glass case and say, "Kirk Cameron gave me this!"

The reason he was ecstatic when he called was that seventy-five extras on the set had each received a copy of "Something to Think About," and no one took offense. He added, "Ray, I was driving around Toronto thinking, *That would be a good place to do an open-air.* He laughed and asked, "What's happening to me?"

Breaking the Sound Barrier

As time passed, Kirk and I began to travel together for ministry. One weekend Kirk, his mom (who loves the Lord), and I went to Ohio for ministry. After the Saturday night meeting, we drove downtown to a festival to preach open-air. On the way there Kirk was tempted to speak, but felt the usual nerves we all feel. When he looked at me and said, "I've got a headache," I audibly prayed that it would go away. After we found an area in the middle of a park, I began speaking and was able to attract a reasonable sized crowd, but after about twenty minutes a police officer told me to stop. When I asked if it was public domain (I knew it was), people in the crowd began calling out, "Let him speak!" The officer became so angry that I thought the veins in his neck were going to burst (and I was going to get arrested), so I asked him if there was someplace else I could preach. He kindly told me where to go.

We found another area about a hundred yards away and began speaking again. This time the atmosphere was much better. I spoke for about ten minutes then turned to Kirk and asked, "Do you want to give your testimony?" He had been thinking at that very moment, *This would be a good time to give my testimony,* and without hesitation jumped up on the box. I immediately went to the sidewalk, stopped groups of strangers, and asked them, "Have you heard of Kirk Cameron, from 'Growing Pains?'" When they said yes, I simply replied, "He's over there speaking"—and they rushed to the crowd like magnets. I was pumped. If I'd had my act together, I would have organized a dozen Christians to do the same thing.

Kirk preached open-air three times that night. His mom even got up and spoke. This was such a big blessing. When we first met, Kirk wouldn't even hand out tracts because he was concerned about his image in Hollywood. If he was painted by the media as a fanatic, it could mean the end of any big movie roles. By open-air preaching, he wasn't just coming out of the closet—he was roaring out of the closet on a motorcycle. He told me later that when I prayed for his headache, it went away immediately. If you are wanting to preach open-air, be ready for some sort of hindering headache, but know that God is only too willing to remove it so that you can preach His gospel.

The Butterfly

Around that time Kirk asked me to join him at a meeting with executives from the movie's production company. We were picked up in a huge, white limousine. As four other men got in the vehicle, Kirk whispered to me who they were. One was the singer/songwriter whose songs include the well-known "Butterfly Kisses," and the others wore wigs that were just as big.

We were driven to a very classy restaurant and were seated at a table that was nothing short of "spiffing" (as the English say). One of the gentlemen began by telling Kirk and me, "I have just seen the second movie—the one where you two worked on the gospel presentation—and it is wonderful!" The man next to him agreed wholeheartedly, much to our joy.

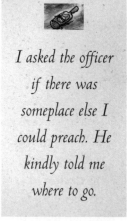

I asked the officer if there was someplace else I could preach. He kindly told me where to go.

I reached down into my bag and saw that I had a "butterfly" tract and decided that we could use it to scare the living daylights out of Mr. Butterfly Kisses (this tract has a printed butterfly that flies out of a card as it's opened). Kirk wrote on the envelope, "We appreciate you, etc.," and decided to give it to him just before dessert. Timing is everything.

A few minutes later our meals were served with a decorative butterfly on both of the plates. Mr. Butterfly...butterfly tract...butterfly meal...It was strange, so I whispered to Kirk that I thought God was going to take this lowly little ministry of ours and cause it to fly.[10]

At the conclusion of the meal we exchanged business cards, and I noticed that across the top of their cards were the words "Butterfly Group." That sent Kirk and I into a spin. (By the way, when he opened the card, Mr. Butterfly jumped and then laughed. Ladies are better—they scream.)

With that encouragement from God, Kirk and I created a three-video series called "The Way of the Master," which contains "Hell's Best Kept Secret," "True and False Conver-sion," and "WDJD?" (What Did Jesus Do?). In the last video, we share the gospel with over a dozen people (including atheists) using the Law. We also wrote a "Left Behind" tract with action pictures from the movie.

Cloud Ten Pictures was so excited about the soul-winning potential of the movie, and Kirk's passion for souls, that soon thereafter Kirk got a call from Peter Lalonde, the CEO of Cloud Ten. He offered to pay for and mail a copy of Kirk's message (in which he preaches the essence of "Hell's Best Kept Secret") to every youth group leader in the country who wants one!

The Master

Kirk received a master of *Left Behind II: Tribulation Force,* but didn't view it because he didn't like to watch himself act. We were both concerned that the editors might for some reason decide to remove the Ten Commandments from the gospel scene, so I couldn't wait until my copy arrived to see if they had left it in.

A few days later I had it in my hands. I was apprehensive as I pushed "Play" on the remote. The movie started off a lit-tle slow, but it wasn't long until I was pulled into the story. The gospel scene was just as it was shot—nothing changed, nothing removed! But more than that, I had forgotten that we had also suggested rewrites for the scene with the two witnesses at the Wailing Wall. Instead of simply preaching grace, we had them quote Old Testament verses about God's omniscience and the fact that He will bring every work to judgment, including every secret thing. Then we had the Rabbi say that he had kept the Commandments from his youth, followed by one of the witnesses telling him that no one will be made right with God by keeping the Law—that we are saved by grace and grace alone (God's unmerited favor). Then came the good news of the cross. I was ecstatic. I shouted for joy and wept at the same time.

A few minutes after the movie ended, Kirk happened to call. I raved big time! He then watched it, and wrote the following in our monthly e-mail newsletter:[11]

> I was initially given a rough cut of the movie, which has 80% of the film cut and scored with temporary music and sound effects. I didn't watch it, and decided to wait for the final version. When Ray and I were sent the final copy from Cloud Ten, he watched it immediately, then told me how much he loved it. Honestly, I was nervous about the final outcome. I so wanted it to be good that I couldn't bring myself to watch it for a week. I finally watched it and was thrilled! Although I'm incredibly critical of any project I work on, I have to say that I believe this movie is better than *Left Behind* Part 1 and certainly has tremendous evangelistic potential. I think you're going to love it.
>
> One thought that comes to mind as I watch the movie is how good some of the acting is. Brad Johnson (who plays Rayford Steele) does an incredible job in the movie witnessing to his pilot buddy, Chris. After listening to the evangelistic words coming out of his mouth, it's hard to believe that Brad is not a Christian. I had the chance to witness to him personally for about an hour as we rehearsed our lines, Ray shared with him for several minutes on different occasions on the set, and Brad's wife is born again. God is incredible—using a non-Christian actor to effectively communicate the gospel of everlasting life to non-Christians like himself. Perhaps when Brad watches the movie, "Rayford" will convince Brad and he'll be saved!

A week or so later, reviews of the movie started pouring in:

> Dr. Jack Van Impe: "I've never seen a Christian film that's its equal. The soul-winning potential of this film is staggering. Millions could be touched by its message."

> Dr. Ted Baehr, Founder, Christian Film and Television Commission: "The evangelistic power of this film is awesome! Characters repeatedly come to Christ in powerfully acted and compelling scenes."

> Randall Murphree, Editor, *American Family Association Journal:* "On a scale of one to ten, it's a ten."

> Tom Saab, Founder and Director, Christian Film Festivals of America, Inc.: "Finally, a superb 'end-times' thriller that can truly be used for evangelism and is guaranteed to lead thousands to a saving knowledge of Jesus Christ. Throughout the film individuals receive Jesus as Lord and Savior in ways that will touch the most stubborn and cynical heart...In addition, the producers, writers, and directors made sure that sin, repentance, and forgiveness were mentioned and they emphasized that acknowledging our sin, turning away from it, and asking God's forgiveness were an essential part of receiving Jesus as Savior and Lord. There are not just a few powerful and moving scenes in this film as most Christian films have, but numerous sequences throughout every part of the movie that will have you crying or cheering, tug at your heart, cause you to think, and definitely inspire you to go out and share the gospel of Jesus Christ with a lost and dying world.

When we were revising the Ten Commandments scene, we had no idea that it was a miracle in the making. But God is like that. He tends to work quietly in our lives.

Perhaps He's working a miracle in your life right now, calling you to boldly step out in faith.

"I'm Going to Explode!"

The first time Kirk called our ministry he had earnestly asked, "How can we get this teaching to the Church?" I answered, "Welcome to Club Frustration. I have been trying to do that for twenty years." His experience was like that of many who understand the importance of the teaching. He would regularly say things like, "I feel like I'm going to explode with this!"

His wife, Chelsea, told me that in January 2003, he was walking around their house, asking how on earth we were going to get this teaching out there and stir the Church into an understanding of the true gospel, when he suddenly dropped to his knees on the kitchen floor, put his hands on his head, looked to the heavens and cried, "How can we get this teaching to the Church?!"

Kirk had appeared on the Trinity Broadcasting Network (TBN) about six weeks earlier, and gave our web site address inviting people to listen to the teaching online. We immediately had 71,000 hits, which crashed the server and brought down 200 other sites. When I called TBN and told them the sad story, they invited both Kirk and I back to their program for a thirty-minute interview.

We purchased our own server and rigged the site so that it wouldn't crash. Kirk said, "I am going to so plead with people to go to the web site and listen to the teaching that I am going to make a fool of myself." Dwight Thompson was scheduled to interview us, so I mailed him a book and tape, urging him to become familiar with the teaching before the interview (it can make or break an interview).

The day of the interview, the program manager at TBN called to say that Dwight Thompson was ill and couldn't do the interview. He asked if Kirk could interview me for thirty minutes, and then host the rest of the two-hour program. After Kirk and I discussed the pros and cons, we suggested that he interview me for fifteen minutes, then preach "Hell's Best Kept Secret" live. The manager said they would be delighted for Kirk to preach, and they even extended the program for an extra thirty minutes so that he wouldn't be pressed for time. Club Frustration disbanded. We were more than ecstatic!

That night two pumped and privileged preachers were praying, planning, and quoting verses of victory on the way to the TBN studio. The first time I ever preached "Hell's Best Kept Secret" I said, "Lord, I will share this teaching a thousand times if You want me to." To that moment, it had been 768 times.

For seven years he had performed live in front of an audience, perhaps to prepare him for this moment.

I sat to one side of Kirk while he shared the teaching in a live broadcast to 124 countries. He was relaxed, passionate, and incredibly focused. For seven years he had performed live in front of an audience for "Growing Pains," perhaps to prepare him for this moment. Each week, 40 million people tuned in for the hit sitcom. He had become a teenage heartthrob and many times people would approach him to say, "I grew up with you." God had chosen to bring this vital teaching through a vessel who had the favor of much of the nation. At the conclusion, he encouraged viewers to visit our web site, www.livingwaters.com.

The next day Living Waters was swamped with orders and phone calls. In fact, we were swamped with more than orders. The local water supply (our neighbors) had released hundreds of thousands of gallons of excess water, so for the first few hours of that day a four-foot-wide, six-inch-deep torrent flowed around Living Waters Ministries. During this time, my son Daniel came into my office and reminded me that that day (January 10) was the fourteen-year anniversary of our arrival in the United States.

TBN called that afternoon and reported that their Nielson rating skyrocketed while Kirk was on. They were overwhelmed. That episode had 22 million viewers in the U.S. and 200 million worldwide. We also had over a million hits on our web site that day, and our server didn't crash.

This is one of the dozens of e-mails that TBN received: "I just received Christ as my Lord and Savior. I feel like I have been running from God my whole life...I really didn't know what it meant and how big of a sinner I really was until to-night...I know I only have one chance to get it right so I don't want to blow it. I have known this for a lifetime but just decided to surrender after stumbling across Kirk on a television show. Thank you for my answered prayers. A new brother in Christ."

A spokesman for TBN said, "I can't believe what is going on. This is the hottest thing to ever hit TBN!" When we asked if they would like us to do a regular program teaching Christians how to share their faith, they said, "How, where, and how quickly can we begin?"

To date, TBN has screened Kirk preaching "Hell's Best Kept Secret" five times. You may like to receive a free e-mail newsletter to keep up with what's happening with our ministry. See www.livingwaters.com to sign up.

CHAPTER 23

THE POWER of HUMOR

As you witness, don't be afraid to use humor to soften a stranger's heart. If you think that you don't have the "gift of humor," we can help you. Go to our web site at www.livingwaters.com and click on "The Power of Humor."

I often use humor when I want to speak with a stranger. As I was flying from Phoenix to California, I was seated next to a young couple. I introduced myself and continued to type on my laptop. As I typed, I noticed out of the corner of my eye that the young lady pulled out a large plastic bottle of water and took a drink. Her husband then held out his hand for the bottle and took a drink. Without looking up, I reached out my hand to take the bottle for my drink. That made them both laugh. We talked a little (and laughed some more), and so I felt at liberty to take a risk. As the plane took off I pressed the button on the man's armrest, causing his seat to go back as we lifted into the air. That sent his wife into hysterics. From then on, both of them were very friendly. I told them about my connection to Kirk, which gave me an entrance into the things of God. I asked, "Are you Christians?" They both told me that they were, but the husband said that he had not been born again. I asked if they thought they were good people. Both did, but he turned out to be a lying, thieving, adulterer at heart. She was a liar, a thief, and a blasphemer. As I talked about the cross, tears welled in their eyes. She said it was amazing that I was speaking to them, because she had just told her husband that they should start going to church. I didn't press for a "decision" from them, but instead encouraged them to seek the Lord in repentance and establish a prayer life together.

If you think that you have to get "decisions" from sinners, you will often be discouraged.

The following day the husband returned an e-mail from me saying that they really appreciated the chat we had. If you see "success" in witnessing as simply faithfully planting the seed of God's Word in the hearts of sinners, then you will find much success. If you think that you have to get "decisions" from sinners, you will often be discouraged.

The Bible says that our ministry is to sow seed. If we sow, someone somewhere will reap. He who sows and he who reaps will rejoice together. He who sows is nothing and he who reaps is nothing, but the glory belongs to God, who causes the seed to grow. Once we understand that, and let God do His work, then we will see sinners come to Christ and "bring forth fruit."

About fifty feet from my office window was a man selling hot dogs. I would pass Mike every day as I went to the courthouse to hand out tracts. One day he stopped me and began to talk. I took the opportunity to go through the Law with him, and then encouraged him to cross the road and take a tour of our ministry some time.

When he came by that afternoon, I showed him around, and as he was leaving he asked if we could talk further about the things of God. We made an appointment for 7:00 the next morning.

When Mike arrived, he made it clear that he wanted to give his life to Jesus Christ. I had him pray, then I prayed for him and gave him some literature. As he was leaving, he stopped at my office door and said, "You have no idea what this has meant to me." He came over later that morning and gave hot dogs to our staff. The question then arose, "Are hot dogs 'fruit'?" We came to the conclusion that they were, and time proved us right.

My Cup Runneth Over

It was 4:30 in the morning. Kirk and I were in South Carolina. The pastor was picking us up at 4:55 a.m. to take us to the airport and Kirk wasn't answering his cell phone. He had apparently slept in! He was fortunate to have me traveling with him. I had done this hundreds of times. Kirk was a comparative novice.

Despite the fact that I was only half dressed, I went across the hall and knocked on his door. I knocked once. Twice. No answer! Suddenly I heard a familiar *click!* My door had shut, leaving me in the hallway, half dressed. No matter. The important thing was to wake up Kirk. I ran down the hallway to the front desk so they could call him.

As I entered the reception area, there was Kirk—fully

dressed, casually drinking a cup of coffee, and witnessing to an officer of the law! Meanwhile, I was half asleep, half dressed, and locked out of my room, and I had three people staring at me as though I were some sort of nut.

A few hours later we were on a plane heading for Los Angeles, with a woman named Hope sitting next to us. Kirk accidentally knocked over his cup of hot coffee onto his lap. What was his reaction as that boiling liquid hit his tender flesh? Did he go, "Man, that hurt!"? Yes, he did. He felt the pain. (I think I've heard that somewhere before.) Actually, he *yelled* with pain. It was a blessing that I was there to help. I quickly grabbed napkins and handed them to him. That's what friends are for. Suddenly, I knocked over my ice water onto my lap. Man, it was cold!

All sign of Hope had gone as soon as Kirk had spilled his coffee. Fortunately she reappeared with a stack of napkins. Hope does not disappoint. We both had wet right legs—his was hot and mine was cold. It reminded us that Jesus said we should be either hot or cold as Christians.

The next time the flight attendant came by to offer us drinks, Hope asked her for a couple of kids' "sippy" cups.

The above incident isn't isolated. I am a walking disaster. If you don't believe it, ask Mark Spence. He often shakes his head in disbelief when he learns what happens to me. If I have a hammer in my hand, my wife gets a Band-Aid (see my book *Comfort, the Feebleminded*). If I build anything, it is bound to collapse (ask my daughter). One day, Jacob (my eldest son) and I went home to load my van with boxes of books from our garage. I backed the vehicle up to the garage door, careful not to knock over any of Sue's potted plants. As we were loading, I noticed that I had come close to the plants, but thankfully hadn't knocked any over.

When we arrived at the ministry and went around to the

back of the van to unload, much to our surprise we found a plant hanging out of the back door of the vehicle. I had slammed the door and taken some extra baggage along—one of Sue's potted plants. Everyone is amazed at how I manage to do things like that so often.

That night Sue and I arrived home and couldn't get up our driveway. It was blocked by a large plant holder. I had managed to drag it the full length of our driveway before ripping out one plant and driving away. Sue wasn't surprised.

Shortly after that, I was asked by a friend to call a key pastor named Bob in a large church. The reason for the call was to make contact for future ministry. The conversation went well. Very well. We laughed, spoke of the things of God, and even talked about our common interest in surfing. He said that he would get back to me, and he sounded very sincere. As the conversation wound down I felt humbly proud of myself. I had left a good impression. However, after he said good-bye, I heard myself conclude, "Bob bless you, God. Bye."

I have mentioned these incidents for a reason. After reading about some of the events in this book, you may get the impression that I'm something I'm not—and if you put anyone up on a pedestal you may find it hard to reach the things they are reaching. *Any* Christian can do the things that I have done, because it is *God* who is at work in each of us. It is a level playing field. The great key to being used by God is to realize that He uses "nobodys" from nowhere, who have nothing to offer Him but a surrendered heart.

I come from a completely normal family. I have an aunt who got into financial difficulties and robbed a bank. That seemed to work well, so she robbed another. Then another. She was caught on the fourth, and got two years in prison. Another aunt moved in with a one-legged Catholic priest. She rode around with him on his motorbike. Nothing so unusual about that, except that he was in his forties and she was in her eighties. My own mom got a new boyfriend who was fifteen years younger than her—when she was pushing eighty. Add to that a smattering of adultery, lesbianism, drugs, suicide, burglary, fornication, divorce, and one con man, and you can see that my relatives are completely normal.

Total Surrender

Recently a young man called to tell me how he was on fire for God. I was surprised because the last time I spoke to him he was a professing Christian, but was deeply depressed and suicidal. When I asked what caused him to turn his life around, he simply said, "Total surrender." He explained that the root of his depression and suicidal thoughts was selfishness. That really is the key. Total surrender. No more selfishness. Slam the door on sin and self, and don't drag along any extra baggage.

Part of total surrender is to know that when the world says you have "rights," you know that you don't have any. They were given up at Calvary. When the world says something that seems to make sense, you filter it through the Word of God, and if it's not in line with Scripture, you throw it out. God's ways are not the ways of the world. Take for instance how I have learned to respond to angry e-mails (we sell millions of tracts each year, and each one lists our web site address). A man named Tony wrote to me and stated, "Hey, thanks for the handout I received at a concert last night." He then said that he had used it in the bathroom, and ended his letter with "Satan loves you!"

I wrote back a simple, "Thanks, Tony. I appreciate you letting us know. God bless, Ray." His response was interesting: "I like your style. You at least follow the teachings of Jesus in your human interactions. I take back the Satan stuff. Peace to you. Tony."

I wrote again to tell him about myself, the area where I lived, etc. When he responded by telling me that he was a professing atheist, I asked if he would like a free copy of *God Doesn't Believe in Atheists*. He did, and he sent me his address. Another e-mail read:

> Hi Ray,
> I was not very pleased to read the !*$&@ about God and Jesus. First of all: Jesus is dead. For almost 2000 years. Why should you pray to a dead man? Second: God is !*$%@. Have you ever seen him? Stupid Americans. Killing each other all day with your guns, people are starving and still believe in that !*$%@. Stop it now, it's a waste of time. Don't ever send me again something about god or j-sus, I hate them. And I hate Muslims too of course.
> Thijs from Holland

I replied:

> Thijs,
> Thanks for taking the time to share your thoughts. Holland is a beautiful land. I was in Amsterdam a couple of years ago. Loved it. Again, thanks for writing.
> Ray

He quickly responded with:

> Hi Ray,
> Thank you too for your nice answer. Happy to hear you like Holland! See you, and sorry for my first e-mail.
> Thijs Scheijvens

We have access to the most powerful of weapons—love. So the next time someone abuses you for your faith, don't react the way you feel like reacting. Instead, think what love would do. Then do it.

I noticed that a rather macho friend of mine lacked verbal expression of love for his wife, so I decided that I would help him. When she called him on his cell phone, he answered with a typical unromantic, "What's up?" I looked at him earnestly and whispered, "I love you…I love you," and gestured to let his wife know that fact. He glanced at me and said, "Ray says he loves you," and without missing a beat, carried on with his conversation.

My friend did love his wife, but love without any expression at all is an oxymoron. It is food with no taste, fire without heat, music without sound. So don't let love be passive. Openly show your love for God and man by making a diligent search for hearts open to the gospel.

Love Fulfills the Law

If we love God with all of our heart, soul, mind, and strength, and love our neighbor as we love ourself, we satisfy the Law. In Romans 13:8–10 we are told:

> Owe no one anything except to love one another, for he who loves another has fulfilled the law. For the commandments, "You shall not commit adultery," "You shall not murder," "You shall not steal," "You shall not bear false witness," "You shall not covet," and if there is any other commandment, are all summed up in this saying, namely, "You shall love your neighbor as yourself." Love does no harm to a neighbor; therefore love is the fulfillment of the law.

In other words, if we love someone we won't covet his goods or his wife. Nor will we lie to him, steal from him, commit adultery with his wife, kill him, or even hate him. That means there would be no theft, no rape, no murder, no prejudice, no violence, no robbery, no greed, no adultery, no lawsuits, etc. How society would change!

Because we as a nation have forsaken God's Law, America is reaping the sad consequences. If we were able to completely fulfill the Law, we wouldn't need civil law. But the more Lawlessness abounds, the more we need civil laws. If a nation fulfills the Law (in Christ), it reaps national harmony instead of the chaos we now see.

With the daily news reports of invading killer bees, killer mosquitoes, killer tornadoes, child killers, kids who kill kids, kids who kill parents, unprecedented droughts, out-of-control fires, horrific murder-suicides, corporate fraud, massive layoffs, falling stocks, and much, much more, and it is no exaggeration to say that America is sick, from sea to shining sea.

Because we as a nation have forsaken God's Law, America is reaping the sad consequences.

Those who know their Bibles suspect that there's more here than meets the eye. They have studied the promised repercussions for the nation of Israel if they didn't abide by certain God-given principles. They then look at the United States and see striking parallels between America and what happened to Israel. For example, Deuteronomy 28 tells us that if the Israelites forsook the Ten Commandments (see Deuteronomy 27), certain terrible things would happen. They would be struck with diseases in their children and in their land. They would be plagued with mildew (mold), terrible drought, horrific and incurable diseases, irrational fears, marriage breakdown, repossession, and bankruptcy. Their children would be taken from them, their crops would be diseased, and aliens would invade their borders.

These were parallels I noticed right through the 1990s. Almost everything lined up—everything, that is, except an invasion by enemies. Deuteronomy warned of that, but that threat appeared to be one that was peculiar to the nation of Israel. It couldn't apply to this country. America was the one and only superpower of the world. No weapon that was formed against us could prosper. Great oceans protected us from any enemy attack—that is, up until September 11, 2001.

Sadly, when the enemy struck our nation, few said that the incident had anything to do with God. We had forsaken the Ten Commandments, sanctioned millions of abortions, loved violence, adultery, pornography, etc., but it was unthinkable that America's sins called for God's chastening hand.

Unfortunately, the conscience of our nation failed to do its duty. In recent years the Church as a whole has been deathly silent when it comes to having a clear evangelistic voice. According to Bill Bright, the founder of Campus Crusade for Christ, only 2 percent of Christians actively share their faith. That means (for some reason) 98 percent don't. But more than that, even many of the 2 percent who share their faith fail to use the Ten Commandments within their sphere of influence. This was the way Jesus presented the gospel (Luke 18:18–22), but most don't follow His example. They instead follow the traditions of modern evangelism, and therefore strip the gospel of its power. If we discard the bow, we shouldn't wonder why the arrow has no thrust.

Consequently the Church's light has been snuffed out in the darkness of the hour in which we live. Its savor has been lost. It has become good for nothing but to be trampled underfoot by men.

The Gospel of Luke diagnoses the nation's disease and thankfully gives us the certain cure. Luke 10:2 tells us what it is. There is a lack of laborers—laborers who have been raised up by God.

We have been obeying the admonition to pray for laborers, and *you* are the answer to our prayers. You are the needed salt and light. We would be bold enough to say that one big step in the right direction is for you to get "The Way of the Master" video series. It has been designed to train you for the job of sharing the gospel. View it for yourself and see how God is using it to equip and enthuse the most lukewarm of Christians. You may even be stirred enough to hold a seminar and screen the series to those who have the unction to show up.

Then again, if we want to reach the lost, we should ask ourselves how much we want true revival. Would our churches be radical enough to change the order of our Sunday morning service and show the series to the church? Perhaps that's asking too much. The order of service is a tradition. To change it and equip the saints is a little too radical—and that may bring about what we profess to be praying for: genuine God-ordained revival.

On the morning I locked myself out of my hotel room and found Kirk sharing the gospel with a policeman, the officer walked out of the doors of the hotel and hollered back, "I'll see you in the movies." Kirk smiled and said, "Yes, but I want to see you in heaven." That's the bottom line. Make sure you are there, and once you have trusted in the Savior, take the light to others who are still sitting in the shadow of death.

Well Done...

While I was boarding a plane, I gave tracts to five Muslim girls. One of them commented, "You look like Einstein!" As they walked passed me on the plane, I heard two of them mumble, "There's Einstein!" After the flight, as they were leaving, the youngest girl (around six years old) walked past me and said, "Good-bye, Frankenstein!"

So, whether you look like Einstein or Frankenstein, be a troublemaker for the kingdom of God. Do something today for your Lord. Go to the highways, the byways, and the hedges, and compel the lost to come in. Pray for divine encounters. Ask God to lead you to *your* MacArthur Park, to *your* 5th Street, or to *your* Santa Monica. Watch out for the goose. Be nice to angry females. Remember that you have Someone with you who will never leave you or forsake you, so rejoice if you get bruised. It is for the most noble of causes that you suffer. Those who are hated by humanity are often heroes of heaven. Live to hear the words, "Well done, good and faithful servant."

Strive to be a *normal* biblical Christian, and whatever you do, stay out of your comfort zone—save that place of ease and safety for eternity.

THE
LOVE TEST

The thought of handing out a gospel tract:
A. Terrifies me.
B. Embarrasses me.
C. Excites me.
D. Bores me.

I believe the person I give the tract to would probably:
A. Take the tract.
B. Physically attack me.
C. Think I'm a fanatic.
D. The question is irrelevant.

A person who dies in his sins will:
A. Be separated from God forever.
B. Go to a Christless eternity.

C. Go to hell forever.

D. Go to heaven.

The fact that anyone could go to hell forever:

A. Doesn't worry me.

B. Concerns me.

C. Horrifies me.

D. Isn't my problem.

I could deal with my fears in giving away tracts if I was given:

A. $20.

B. $100.

C. $1,000.

D. A promise that God would be with me.

In Colossians 1:28, we are told that we should be warning:

A. All Jews.

B. Our relatives.

C. Every person.

D. Every Christian.

In the light of this command, I am:

A. Disobedient.

B. Faithful.

C. Unfaithful.

D. Complacent.

I am:

A. An on-fire Christian who will use any legitimate means to reach the lost.

B. Questioning if I really love God.

C. Lukewarm (see Revelation 3:16).

D. Deceived about my state before God.

If I am anything but an on-fire (biblical) Christian who will use any legitimate means to reach the lost, I will:
A. Ignore this test.
B. Repent before God and seek to reach the lost.
C. Become more religious.
D. Distract myself with other things.

END NOTES

1. Manmade "religion" doesn't deal with the issue of man's sinful heart. It merely puts lipstick on the pig.

2. This is a common denominator in much of demonic possession. See Ephesians 6:1–3.

3. See *Revival's Golden Key* (Bridge-Logos Publishers) for details.

4. For more comprehensive teaching on this subject, see *Hell's Best Kept Secret* (Whitaker House) and *Revival's Golden Key* (Bridge-Logos Publishers).

5. This sequence has been included in the video "In Season, Out of Season." To order, see www.livingwaters.com or call 800-437-1893.

6. See our video/DVD, "Open-Air Preaching From A–Z."

7. For the full encounter, see *How to Win Souls and Influence People* (Bridge-Logos Publishers).

8. The video, *BC-AD: Barrier-Comfort Atheism Debate*, is available through Living Waters Publications, 800-437-1893 or www.livingwaters.com.

9. Listen to Kirk Cameron share this teaching on www.livingwaters.com.

10. A few weeks later we received an e-mail from a woman who had heard about this incident. She said that she went for a walk and specifically asked God if she should add Kirk and me to her prayer list. As she prayed, a butterfly hit her in the head. Then another one did the same thing.

11. Freely available at www.livingwaters.com.

SCHOOL OF BIBLICAL EVANGELISM

If you would like to learn how to effectively share your faith, check out our School of Biblical Evangelism at www.living-waters.com. Here are some commendations from students:

"The School is absolutely awesome; I have been truly blessed by this ministry." **Pastor Brent Wisdom (CA)**

"I cannot explain how blessed I get every time I open the School of Evangelism and study. I have pastored for almost eleven years and have never been to Bible School. Until now! Thank you so much for this great work." **Pastor Wayne Andres (MD)**

"SOBE is opening a completely new world of understanding regarding the gospel and God working in people's lives." **Rick Todd (SC)**

"I am 42 and have shared my belief in Christ for almost 20 years but I have never seen anything as powerful as the teaching I have received from the School of Biblical Evangelism." **James W. Smith (TX)**

"As a graduate of EE and every other evangelism course I can find, yours by far has been the best." **Bill Lawson (NY)**

"I consider this to be the greatest Biblical learning experience of my life." **Steven R. Harbaugh (IN)**